America's Three Constitutions

THE LOCHLAINN SEABROOK COLLECTION

CONSTITUTIONAL HISTORY
America's Three Constitutions: Complete Texts of the Articles of Confederation, U.S. Constitution, and C.S. Constitution
The Articles of Confederation Explained: A Clause-by-Clause Study of America's First Constitution
The Constitution of the Confederate States of America Explained: A Clause-by-Clause Study of the South's Magna Carta

VICTORIAN CONFEDERATE LITERATURE
Rise Up and Call Them Blessed: Victorian Tributes to the Confederate Soldier, 1861-1901
Support Your Local Confederate: Wit and Humor in the Southern Confederacy
The God of War: Nathan Bedford Forrest As He Was Seen By His Contemporaries
The Old Rebel: Robert E. Lee As He Was Seen By His Contemporaries
Victorian Confederate Poetry: The Southern Cause in Verse, 1861-1901

ABRAHAM LINCOLN
Abraham Lincoln: The Southern View - Demythologizing America's Sixteenth President
Lincolnology: The Real Abraham Lincoln Revealed in His Own Words - A Study of Lincoln's Suppressed, Misinterpreted, and Forgotten Writings and Speeches
Lincoln's War: The Real Cause, the Real Winner, the Real Loser
The Great Impersonator! 99 Reasons to Dislike Abraham Lincoln
The Unholy Crusade: Lincoln's Legacy of Destruction in the American South
The Unquotable Abraham Lincoln: The President's Quotes They Don't Want You To Know!

NATURAL HISTORY
North America's Amazing Mammals: An Encyclopedia for the Whole Family
The Concise Book of Owls: A Guide to Nature's Most Mysterious Birds
The Concise Book of Tigers: A Guide to Nature's Most Remarkable Cats

PARANORMAL
Carnton Plantation Ghost Stories: True Tales of the Unexplained from Tennessee's Most Haunted Civil War House!
UFOs and Aliens: The Complete Guidebook

FAMILY HISTORIES
The Blakeneys: An Etymological, Ethnological, and Genealogical Study - Uncovering the Mysterious Origins of the Blakeney Family and Name
The Caudills: An Etymological, Ethnological, and Genealogical Study - Exploring the Name and National Origins of a European-American Family
The McGavocks of Carnton Plantation: A Southern History - Celebrating One of Dixie's Most Noble Confederate Families and Their Tennessee Home

MIND, BODY, SPIRIT
Autobiography of a Non-Yogi: A Scientist's Journey From Hinduism to Christianity (Dr. Amitava Dasgupta, with Lochlainn Seabrook)
Britannia Rules: Goddess-Worship in Ancient Anglo-Celtic Society - An Academic Look at the United Kingdom's Matricentric Spiritual Past
Christ Is All and In All: Rediscovering Your Divine Nature and the Kingdom Within
Christmas Before Christianity: How the Birthday of the "Sun" Became the Birthday of the "Son"
Jesus and the Gospel of Q: Christ's Pre-Christian Teachings As Recorded in the New Testament
Jesus and the Law of Attraction: The Bible-Based Guide to Creating Perfect Health, Wealth, and Happiness Following Christ's Simple Formula
Seabrook's Bible Dictionary of Traditional and Mystical Christian Doctrines
The Bible and the Law of Attraction: 99 Teachings of Jesus, the Apostles, and the Prophets
The Book of Kelle: An Introduction to Goddess-Worship and the Great Celtic Mother-Goddess Kelle, Original Blessed Lady of Ireland
The Goddess Dictionary of Words and Phrases: Introducing a New Core Vocabulary for the Women's Spirituality Movement
Vintage Southern Cookbook: Delicious Dishes From Dixie

WOMEN
Aphrodite's Trade: The Hidden History of Prostitution Unveiled
Princess Diana: Modern Day Moon-Goddess - A Psychoanalytical and Mythological Look at Diana Spencer's Life, Marriage, and Death (with Dr. Jane Goldberg)
Women in Gray: A Tribute to the Ladies Who Supported the Southern Confederacy

REPRINTS
A Short History of the Confederate States of America (author Jefferson Davis; editor Lochlainn Seabrook)
Prison Life of Jefferson Davis (author John J. Craven; editor Lochlainn Seabrook)
Life of Beethoven (author Ludwig Nohl; editor Lochlainn Seabrook)
The New Revelation (author Arthur Conan Doyle; editor Lochlainn Seabrook)

*Lochlainn Seabrook does not author books for fame and fortune,
but for the love of writing and sharing his knowledge.*

SeaRavenPress.com

Warning:

SEA RAVEN PRESS BOOKS WILL EXPAND YOUR ★ MIND!

America's Three Constitutions

COMPLETE TEXTS OF THE
Articles of Confederation, U.S. Constitution, & C.S. Constitution

★ *With Supplemental Documents* ★

CONCEIVED, COLLECTED, ARRANGED, & EDITED WITH AN INTRODUCTION BY THE AUTHOR,
"THE VOICE OF THE TRADITIONAL SOUTH," COLONEL

Lochlainn Seabrook

JEFFERSON DAVIS HISTORICAL GOLD MEDAL WINNER

Diligently Researched and Generously Illustrated for the Elucidation of the Reader

2021

Sea Raven Press, Nashville, Tennessee, USA

AMERICA'S THREE CONSTITUTIONS

Published by
Sea Raven Press, Cassidy Ravensdale, President
PO Box 1484, Spring Hill, Tennessee 37174-1484 USA
SeaRavenPress.com • searavenpress@gmail.com

SEA RAVEN PRESS
SOUTHERN BOOKS, REAL HISTORY!

1ˢᵗ SRP paperback edition, 1ˢᵗ printing, June 2021 • ISBN: 978-1-955351-04-1
1ˢᵗ SRP hardcover edition, 1ˢᵗ printing, June 2021 • ISBN: 978-1-955351-05-8

ISBN: 978-1-955351-04-1 (paperback)
Library of Congress Control Number: 2021940036

America's Three Constitutions: The Complete Texts of the Articles of Confederation, U.S. Constitution, and C.S. Constitution, by Lochlainn Seabrook. Includes an introduction, illustrations, index, endnotes, appendices, and bibliography.

Front and back cover design and art, book design, layout, and interior art by Lochlainn Seabrook. All images, image captions, graphic design, & graphic art copyright © Lochlainn Seabrook. All images selected, placed, manipulated, and/or created by Lochlainn Seabrook. Image cleaning, coloration, & tinting by Lochlainn Seabrook. Cover image: American Colonial Rebel Girl, Virginia, 1777

All persons who approve of the authority and principles of Colonel Lochlainn Seabrook's literary work, and realize its benefits as a means of reeducating the world about the South and the Confederacy, are hereby requested to avidly recommend his books to others and to vigorously cooperate in extending their reach, scope, and influence around the globe.

The views expressed in this book are those of the publisher.

PRINTED & MANUFACTURED IN OCCUPIED TENNESSEE, FORMER CONFEDERATE STATES OF AMERICA

SEA RAVEN PRESS

Dedication

To my patriotic Colonial and Confederate ancestors who fought in both the first (1775) and second (1861) American Revolutionary Wars.

Epigraph

"Our Constitution was made only for a moral and religious people. It is wholly inadequate to the government of any other."

JOHN ADAMS

Second President of the United States under the U.S. Constitution,

IN A LETTER TO THE OFFICERS OF THE FIRST BRIGADE OF THE THIRD DIVISION
OF THE MILITIA OF MASSACHUSETTS, OCTOBER 11, 1798

Contents

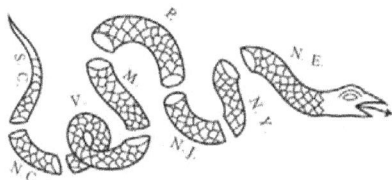

JOIN, or DIE.

Keep Your Body, Mind, & Spirit Vibrating at Their Highest Level

YOU CAN DO SO BY READING THE BOOKS OF

SEA RAVEN PRESS

There is nothing that will so perfectly keep your body, mind, and spirit in a healthy condition as to think wisely and positively. Hence you should not only read this book, but also the other books that we offer. They will quicken your physical, mental, and spiritual vibrations, enabling you to maintain a position in society as a healthy erudite person.

KEEP YOURSELF WELL-INFORMED!

The well-informed person is always at the head of the procession, while the ignorant, the lazy, and the unthoughtful hang onto the rear. If you are a Spiritual man or woman, do yourself a great favor: read Sea Raven Press books and stay well posted on the Truth. It is almost criminal for one to remain in ignorance while the opportunity to gain knowledge is open to all at a nominal price.

We invite you to visit our Webstore for a wide selection of wholesome, family-friendly, well-researched, educational books for all ages. You will be glad you did!

Five-Star Books & Gifts From the Heart of the American South

SeaRavenPress.com

LochlainnSeabrook.com
BestCivilWarBookEver.com
NathanBedfordForrestBooks.com

Notes to the Reader

THE TWO MAIN POLITICAL PARTIES IN 1860

☞ As this book touches on the topic of the War for Southern Independence (1861), and as that conflict is deeply connected to the American Revolutionary War (1775), it is germane to note the following. In any study of America's Victorian antebellum, bellum, and postbellum periods, it is vitally important to understand that in 1860 the two major political parties—the Democrats and the newly formed Republicans—were the opposite of what they are today. In other words, the Democrats of the mid 19th Century were Conservatives, akin to the Republican Party of today, while the Republicans of the mid 19th Century were Liberals, akin to the Democratic Party of today.[1]

The author's cousin, Confederate Vice President and Democrat Alexander H. Stephens: a Southern Conservative.

Thus the Confederacy's Democratic president, Jefferson Davis, was a Conservative (with libertarian leanings); the Union's Republican president, Abraham Lincoln, was a Liberal (with socialistic leanings).[2] This is why, in the mid 1800s, the conservative wing of the Democratic Party was known as "the States' Rights Party."[3]

Hence, the Democrats of the Civil War period referred to themselves as "conservatives," "confederates," "anti-centralists," or "constitutionalists" (the latter because they favored strict adherence to the original Constitution—which tacitly guaranteed states' rights—as created by the Founding Fathers), while the Civil War Republicans called themselves "liberals," "nationalists," "centralists," or "consolidationists" (the latter three because they wanted to nationalize the central government and consolidate political power in Washington, D.C.).[4] In 1889 President Davis, who referred to the 1860 Democrats as "the conservative power of the country,"[5] himself explained the political situation at the time this way:

> . . . the names adopted by political parties in the United States have not always been strictly significant of their principles. In general terms it may be said that the old Federal party [Liberal] inclined to nationalism [then a term for big government], or consolidation [that is, consolidation of power in the Federal government], and that the Whig party [liberalistic], which succeeded it, although not identical with it, was favorable, in the main, to a strong Central Government [liberalism and socialism]. On the other hand, its opponent, the Republican [Conservative], afterward known as the Democratic party [until the election of 1896, when the two parties reversed, becoming the parties we know today], was dominated by the idea of the sovereignty of the States and the federal or confederate character of the Union [Americanism or conservatism]. Although other elements have entered into its organization at different periods, this has been its vital, cardinal, and abiding principle.[6]

Since this idea is new to most of my readers, let us further demystify it by viewing it from the perspective of the American Revolutionary War. If Davis and his conservative Southern constituents (the Democrats of 1861) had been alive in 1775, they would have sided with George Washington and the American colonists, who sought to secede from the tyrannical government of Great Britain; if Lincoln and his Liberal Northern constituents (the Republicans of 1861) had been alive at that time, they would have sided with King George III and the English monarchy, who sought to maintain the American colonies as possessions of the British Empire. It is due to this very comparison that we Southerners often refer to our secession from the U.S. as the Second Declaration of Independence and the "Civil War" as the Second American Revolutionary War.

Without a basic understanding of these facts, the American "Civil War" will forever remain incomprehensible. For a full discussion of this topic see my book, *Abraham Lincoln Was a Liberal, Jefferson Davis Was a Conservative: The Missing Key to Understanding the American Civil War*.

A WORD ON EARLY AMERICAN MATERIAL

☛ In order to preserve the authentic historicity of the antebellum, bellum, and postbellum periods, I have retained the original spellings, formatting, and punctuation of the early Americans I quote. These include such items as British-English spellings, long-running paragraphs, obsolete words, and various literary devices peculiar to the time. However, I have corrected misspelled names to prevent confusion, and also *where possible*, inaccurate dates and locations (the inevitable result of old faulty memories). Bracketed words within quotes are my additions and clarifications, while italicized words within quotes are (where indicated) my emphasis.

PRESENTISM

☛ As a historian I view *presentism* (judging the past according to present day mores and customs) as the enemy of authentic history. And this is precisely why the Left employs it in its ongoing war against traditional American, conservative, and Christian values. By looking at history through the lens of modern day beliefs—and,

Judging our ancestors by our own standards is dishonest, unfair, unjust, misleading, and unethical.

just as heinous, fabricating obviously fake history based on emotion, opinion, and political ideology—they are able to distort, revise, and reshape the past into a false narrative that fits their ideological agenda: the liberalization *and* Northernization of America, the enlargement and further centralization of the national government, and total control of American political, economic, and social power, the same agenda that Lincoln championed.[7]

This book rejects presentism and replaces it with what I call *historicalism*: judging our ancestors based on the values of their own time.

To get the most from this work the reader is invited to reject presentism as well. In this way—along with casting aside preconceived notions and the fake history churned out by our left-wing education system—the truth in this work will be most readily ascertained and absorbed; truth that has been rigorously researched and forensically uncovered by myself using the scientific method. As Confederate Colonel Bennett H. Young noted in 1901:

> History is valuable only as it is true. Opinions concerning acts are not history; acts themselves alone are historic.[8]

CONTINUE YOUR AMERICAN HISTORY EDUCATION
☞ American history can never be fully understood without a thorough knowledge of the South's perspective. As this book is only meant to be a brief introductory guide to a single branch of this topic, one cannot hope to learn the complete story here. For those who are interested in additional material from Dixie's viewpoint, please see my comprehensive histories listed on pages 2 and 3.

Introduction

EVERYONE SHOULD HAVE PHYSICAL ACCESS to the three most important conservative documents in American history: The Articles of Confederation, the Constitution of the United States of America, and the Constitution of the Confederate States of America. Unfortunately, most of what is distributed to the public concerning our three magnificent charters has been compiled and issued by Left-wing Constitution-hating editors and publishers—typical grim progressives who are more interested in promoting their failed socialist and communist policies than historical facts.

I believe that the public deserves better than this, and my little book, *America's Three Constitutions*, is the result.

As a Conservative I feel it is only right that these three vital papers should be made available in a pure, unedited, unabridged, unredacted, unrevised format—without the guileful tampering, unreliable misinformation, and misleading disinformation that accompanies most Left-wing publications.

To this end, I have retained the original wording, spelling, and format of each document, preserving the intent and tone of our constitutions' 18th- and 19th-Century authors. I have also written a brief fact sheet for each document that will help guide the reader through the complicated sociopolitical maze we call American history (made all the more hazardous and confusing by the mountains of fake history churned out daily by gaslighting Liberals and unwitting indoctrinated conservatives).

This book is not intended to be an in-depth examination of our three constitutions. The workings of the U.S. Constitution have been exhaustively covered by others, while my popular books, *The Articles of Confederation Explained* and *The Constitution of the Confederate States of America Explained*, thoroughly cover the other two. Rather, this volume is meant to be a type of "pocket constitution," one that puts America's most critical political writings at one's fingertips for both quick reference and in-depth analysis. Buttressing these works, I have included, in chronological order, eight appendices containing additional crucial conservative American documents. These cover the periods before, during, and after our constitutions were penned, giving indispensable historical context as to how our country became the grand "confederate republic" (as Conservative George Washington called the U.S.) that it is today.

I encourage my readers to diligently study the documents I have selected for inclusion in *America's Three Constitutions*. The revolutionary conservative concepts found in these papers changed the world. They will change you too.

Lochlainn Seabrook
Nashville, Tennessee, USA
June 2021
In Nobis Regnat Christus

SEA RAVEN PRESS
NASHVILLE ❦ TENNESSEE
EST. 1995

"Books invite all; they constrain none."
Hartley Burr Alexander (1873-1939)

AMERICA'S
FIRST
CONSTITUTION

Articles of

Confederation

DON'T TREAD ON ME

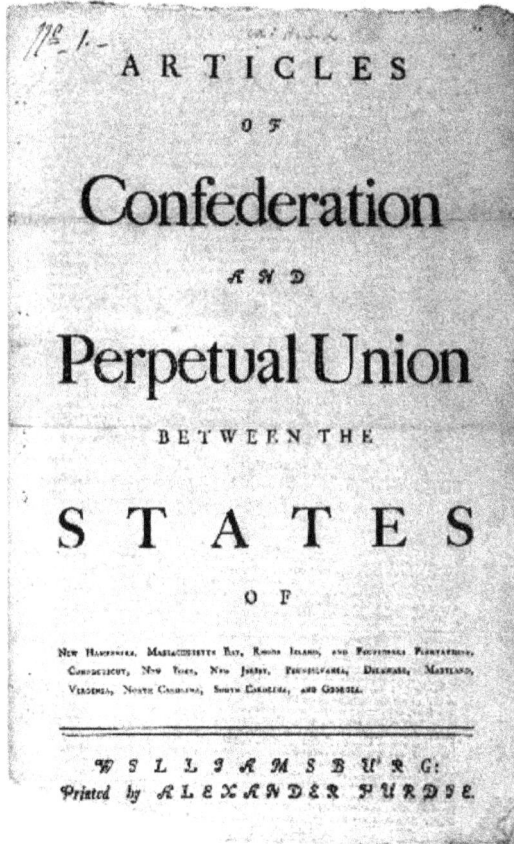

COVER PAGE OF THE ARTICLES OF CONFEDERATION; PUBLISHED BY ALEXANDER PURDIE AT WILLIAMSBURG, VIRGINIA, 1777.

Articles of Confederation
& Perpetual Union
Between the States

☞ The Articles of Confederation were written in response to the Lee Resolution, June 7, 1776. (See Appendix B.)

☞ The first draft of the Articles was drawn up on July 12, 1776.

☞ The Articles were adopted by the Continental Congress on November 15, 1777.

☞ The Articles were signed and ratified by eight colonies on July 9, 1778.

☞ The Articles were ratified by Maryland, the last of the 13 colonies on March 1, 1781.

☞ The principal writer of the Articles was John Dickinson of Delaware.

☞ A contributor to the writing of the Articles was Josiah Bartlett of New Hampshire.

☞ As the Articles of Confederation itself declares, it formed a *"confederacy"*: an informal "league of friendship" between the colonies or states; that is, a *Confederate States of America*, which, in fact, became the nickname of the U.S. early on. A confederacy is defined as a country comprised of loosely associated sovereign nation-states with strong state governments, and a restricted weak national government. Due to these conservative qualities, the Articles were highly favored by colonial Conservatives (like Thomas Paine) but disliked by colonial Liberals (like Alexander Hamilton)—political tumult that would lead to the Articles being replaced by the U.S. Constitution on March 4, 1789.

☞ Some 80 years after the writing of the Articles, Southerners, impatient with the ongoing oppressive and tyrannical leadership of Northern Liberals, sought a revival of the pristine conservatism that existed during the time of the Articles and the period of confederation (1781-1789). This could only be accomplished by secession from the Union, however, which began in 1860. The formation of the *Southern* version of the original Confederate States of America followed.

Life Span of the Articles of Confederation: 1781-1789

T O ALL TO WHOM THESE Presents shall come,

We, the undersigned Delegates of the States affixed to our Names send greeting.

Whereas the Delegates of the United States of America, in Congress assembled, did, on the 15th day of November, in the Year of Our Lord One thousand Seven Hundred and Seventy seven, and in the Second Year of the Independence of America, agree to certain articles of Confederation and perpetual Union between the States of New Hampshire, Massachusetts-bay, Rhode Island and Providence Plantations, Connecticut, New York, New Jersey, Pennsylvania, Delaware, Maryland, Virginia, North-Carolina, South-Carolina, and Georgia.

ARTICLE 1. The Stile of this confederacy shall be, "The United States of America."

JOHN DICKINSON.

ARTICLE 2. Each state retains its sovereignty, freedom and independence, and every Power, Jurisdiction and right, which is not by this confederation expressly delegated to the United States, in Congress assembled.

ARTICLE 3. The said states hereby severally enter into a firm league of friendship with each other, for their common defence, the security of their Liberties, and their mutual and general welfare, binding themselves to assist each other, against all force offered to, or attacks made upon them, or any of them, on account of religion, sovereignty, trade, or any other pretence whatever.

ARTICLE 4, CLAUSE 1. The better to secure and perpetuate mutual friendship and intercourse among the people of the different states in this union, the free inhabitants of each of these states, paupers, vagabonds and fugitives from Justice excepted, shall be entitled to all privileges and immunities of free citizens in the several states; and the people of each state shall have free ingress and regress to and from any other state, and shall enjoy therein all the privileges of trade and commerce, subject to the same duties, impositions and restrictions as the inhabitants thereof respectively, provided that such restrictions shall not extend so far as to prevent the removal of property imported into any state, to any other State of which the Owner is an inhabitant; provided also that no imposition, duties or restriction shall be laid by any state, on the property of the united states, or either of them.

CLAUSE 2. If any Person guilty of, or charged with, treason, felony, or other high misdemeanor in any state, shall flee from Justice, and be found in any of the united states, he shall upon demand of the Governor or executive power of the state from which he fled, be delivered up, and removed to the state having jurisdiction of his offence.

CLAUSE 3. Full faith and credit shall be given in each of these states to the records, acts and judicial proceedings of the courts and magistrates of every other state.

ARTICLE 5, CLAUSE 1. For the more convenient management of the general interests of the united states, delegates shall be annually appointed in such manner as the legislature of each state shall direct, to meet in Congress on the first Monday in November, in every year, with a power reserved to each state to recall its delegates, or any of them, at any time within the year, and to send others in their stead, for the remainder of the Year.

CLAUSE 2. No State shall be represented in Congress by less than two, nor by more than seven Members; and no person shall be capable of being delegate for more than three years, in any term of six years; nor shall any person, being a delegate, be capable of holding any office under the united states, for which he, or another for his benefit receives any salary, fees or emolument of any kind.

CLAUSE 3. Each State shall maintain its own delegates in a meeting of the states, and while they act as members of the committee of the states.

CLAUSE 4. In determining questions in the united states, in Congress assembled, each state shall have one vote.

CLAUSE 5. Freedom of speech and debate in Congress shall not be impeached or questioned in any Court, or place out of Congress, and the members of congress shall be protected in their persons from arrests and imprisonments, during the time of their going to and from, and attendance on congress, except for treason, felony, or breach of the peace.

ARTICLE 6, CLAUSE 1. No State, without the Consent of the united states, in congress assembled, shall send any embassy to, or receive any embassy from, or enter into any conferrence, agreement, alliance, or treaty, with any King prince or state; nor shall any person holding any office of profit or trust under the united states, or any of them, accept of any present, emolument, office, or title of any kind whatever, from any king, prince, or foreign state; nor shall the united states, in congress assembled, or any of them, grant any title of nobility.

AMERICAN REVOLUTIONARY OFFICER GENERAL JOHN SULLIVAN.

CLAUSE 2. No two or more states shall enter into any treaty, confederation, or alliance whatever between them, without the consent of the united states, in congress assembled, specifying accurately the purposes for which the same is to be entered into, and how long it shall continue.

CLAUSE 3. No State shall lay any imposts or duties, which may interfere with any stipulations in treaties, entered into by the united States in congress assembled, with any king, prince, or State, in pursuance of any treaties already proposed by congress, to the courts of France and Spain.

CLAUSE 4. No vessels of war shall be kept up in time of peace, by any state, except such number only, as shall be deemed necessary by the united states, in congress assembled, for the defence of such state, or its trade; nor shall any body of forces be kept up, by any state, in time of peace, except such number only as, in the judgment of the united states, in congress assembled, shall be deemed requisite to garrison the forts necessary for the defence of such state; but every state shall always keep up a well regulated and disciplined militia, sufficiently armed and accounted, and shall provide and constantly have ready for use, in public stores, a due number of field pieces and tents, and a proper quantity of arms, ammunition, and camp equipage.

CLAUSE 5. No State shall engage in any war without the consent of the united states in congress assembled, unless such State be actually invaded by enemies, or shall have received certain advice of a resolution being formed by some nation of Indians to invade such State, and the danger is so imminent as not to admit of a delay till the united states in congress assembled, can be consulted: nor shall any state grant commissions to any ships or vessels of war, nor letters of marque or reprisal, except it be after a declaration of war by the united states in congress assembled, and then only against the kingdom or State, and the subjects thereof, against which war has been so declared, and under such regulations as shall be established by the united states in congress assembled, unless such state be infested by pirates, in which case vessels of war may be fitted out for that occasion, and kept so long as the danger shall continue, or until the united states in congress assembled shall determine otherwise.

ARTICLE 7. When land forces are raised by any state, for the common defence, all officers of or under the rank of colonel, shall be appointed by the legislature of each state respectively by whom such forces shall be raised, or in such manner as such state shall direct, and all vacancies shall be filled up by the state which first made appointment.

ARTICLE 8. All charges of war, and all other expenses that shall be incurred for the common defence or general welfare, and allowed by the united states in congress assembled, shall be defrayed out of a common treasury, which shall be supplied by the several states, in proportion to the value of all land within each state, granted to or surveyed for any Person, as such land and the buildings and improvements thereon shall be estimated, according to such mode as the united states, in congress assembled, shall, from time to time, direct and appoint. The taxes for paying that proportion shall be laid and levied by the authority and direction of the legislatures of the several states within the time agreed upon by the united states in congress assembled.

ARTICLE 9, CLAUSE 1. The united states, in congress assembled, shall have the sole and exclusive right and power of determining on peace and war, except in the cases mentioned in the sixth article - of sending and receiving ambassadors - entering into treaties and alliances, provided that no treaty of commerce shall be made, whereby the legislative power of the respective states shall be restrained from imposing such imposts and duties on foreigners, as their own people are subjected to, or from prohibiting the exportation or importation of any species of goods or commodities whatsoever - of establishing rules for deciding, in all cases, what captures on land or water shall be legal, and in what manner prizes taken by land or naval forces in the service of the united Sates, shall be divided or appropriated - of granting letters of marque and reprisal in times of peace - appointing courts for the trial of piracies and felonies committed on the high seas; and establishing courts; for receiving and determining finally appeals in all cases of captures; provided that no member of congress shall be appointed a judge of any of the said courts.

CLAUSE 2. The united states, in congress assembled, shall also be the last resort on appeal, in all disputes and differences now subsisting, or that hereafter may arise between two or more states concerning boundary, jurisdiction, or any other cause whatever; which authority shall always be exercised in the manner following. Whenever the legislative or executive authority, or lawful agent of any state in controversy with another, shall present a petition to congress, stating the matter in question, and praying for a hearing, notice thereof shall be given, by order of congress, to the legislative or executive authority of the other state in controversy, and a day assigned for the appearance of the parties by their lawful agents, who shall then be directed to appoint, by joint consent, commissioners or judges to constitute a court for hearing and determining the matter in question: but if they cannot agree, congress shall name three persons out of each of the united states, and from the list of such persons each party shall alternately strike out one, the petitioners beginning, until the number shall be reduced to thirteen; and from that number not less than seven, nor more than nine names, as congress shall direct, shall, in the presence of congress, be drawn out by lot, and the persons whose names shall be so drawn, or any five of them, shall be commissioners or judges, to hear and finally determine the controversy, so always as a major part of the judges, who shall hear the cause, shall agree in the determination: and if either party shall neglect to attend at the day appointed, without showing reasons which congress shall judge sufficient, or being present, shall refuse to strike, the congress shall proceed to nominate three persons out of each State, and the secretary of congress shall strike in behalf of such party absent or refusing; and the judgment and sentence of the court, to be appointed in the manner before prescribed, shall be final and conclusive; and if any of the parties shall refuse to submit to the authority of such court, or to appear or defend their claim or cause, the court shall nevertheless proceed to pronounce sentence, or judgment, which shall in like manner be final and decisive; the judgment or sentence and other proceedings being in either case transmitted to congress, and lodged

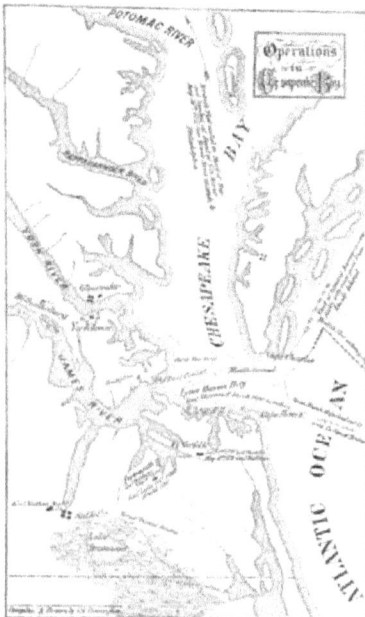

MAP OF REVOLUTIONARY MILITARY OPERATIONS IN CHESAPEAKE BAY.

among the acts of congress, for the security of the parties concerned: provided that every commissioner, before he sits in judgment, shall take an oath to be administered by one of the judges of the supreme or superior court of the State where the cause shall be tried, "well and truly to hear and determine the matter in question, according to the best of his judgment, without favour, affection, or hope of reward": provided, also, that no State shall be deprived of territory for the benefit of the united states.

CLAUSE 3. All controversies concerning the private right of soil claimed under different grants of two or more states, whose jurisdictions as they may respect such lands, and the states which passed such grants are adjusted, the said grants or either of them being at the same time claimed to have originated antecedent to such settlement of jurisdiction, shall, on the petition of either party to the congress of the united states, be finally determined, as near as may be, in the same manner as is before prescribed for deciding disputes respecting territorial jurisdiction between different states.

CLAUSE 4. The united states, in congress assembled, shall also have the sole and exclusive right and power of regulating the alloy and value of coin struck by their own authority, or by that of the respective states - fixing the standard of weights and measures throughout the united states - regulating the trade and managing all affairs with the Indians, not members of any of the states; provided that the legislative right of any state, within its own limits, be not infringed or violated - establishing and regulating post-offices from one state to another, throughout all the united states, and exacting such postage on the papers passing through the same, as may be requisite to defray the expenses of the said office - appointing all officers of the land forces in the service of the united States, excepting regimental officers - appointing all the officers of the naval forces, and commissioning all officers whatever in the service of the united states; making rules for the government and regulation of the said land and naval forces, and directing their operations.

CLAUSE 5. The united states, in congress assembled, shall have authority to appoint a committee, to sit in the recess of congress, to be denominated, "A Committee of the States," and to consist of one delegate from each State; and to appoint such other committees and civil officers as may be necessary for managing the general affairs of the united states under their direction - to appoint one of their number to preside; provided that no person be allowed to serve in the office of president more than one year in any term of three years; to ascertain the necessary sums of money to be raised for the service of the united states, and to appropriate and apply the same for defraying the public expenses; to borrow money or emit bills on the credit of the united states, transmitting every half year to the respective states an account of the sums of money so borrowed or emitted, - to build and equip a navy - to agree upon the number of land forces, and to make requisitions from each state for its quota, in proportion to the number of white inhabitants in such state, which requisition shall be binding; and thereupon the legislature of each state shall appoint the regimental officers, raise the men, and clothe, arm, and equip them, in a soldier-like manner, at the expense of the united states; and the officers and men so clothed, armed, and equipped, shall march to the place appointed, and within the time agreed on by the united states, in congress assembled; but if the united states, in congress assembled, shall, on consideration of circumstances, judge proper that any state should not raise men, or should raise a smaller number than its quota, and that any other state should raise a greater number of men than the quota thereof, such extra number shall be raised, officered, clothed,

THE MINUTE MAN.

armed, and equipped in the same manner as the quota of such state, unless the legislature of such state shall judge that such extra number cannot be safely spared out of the same, in which case they shall raise, officer, clothe, arm, and equip, as many of such extra number as they judge can be safely spared. And the officers and men so clothed, armed, and equipped, shall march to the place appointed, and within the time agreed on by the united states in congress assembled.

CLAUSE 6. The united states, in congress assembled, shall never engage in a war, nor grant letters of marque and reprisal in time of peace, nor enter into any treaties or alliances, nor coin money, nor regulate the value thereof nor ascertain the sums and expenses necessary for the defence and welfare of the united states, or any of them, nor emit bills, nor borrow money on the credit of the united states, nor appropriate money, nor agree upon the number of vessels of war to be built or purchased, or the number of land or sea forces to be raised, nor appoint a commander in chief of the army or navy, unless nine states assent to the same, nor shall a question on any other point, except for adjourning from day to day, be determined, unless by the votes of a majority of the united states in congress assembled.

CLAUSE 7. The congress of the united states shall have power to adjourn to any time within the year, and to any place within the united states, so that no period of adjournment be for a longer duration than the space of six Months, and shall publish the Journal of their proceedings monthly, except such parts thereof relating to treaties, alliances, or military operations, as in their judgment require secrecy; and the yeas and nays of the delegates of each State, on any question, shall be entered on the Journal, when it is desired by any delegate; and the delegates of a State, or any of them, at his or their request, shall be furnished with a transcript of the said Journal, except such parts as are above excepted, to lay before the legislatures of the several states.

ARTICLE 10. The committee of the states, or any nine of them, shall be authorized to execute, in the recess of congress, such of the powers of congress as the united states, in congress assembled, by the consent of nine states, shall, from time to time, think expedient to vest them with; provided that no power be delegated to the said committee, for the exercise of which, by the articles of confederation, the voice of nine states, in the congress of the united states assembled, is requisite.

ARTICLE 11. Canada acceding to this confederation, and joining in the measures of the united states, shall be admitted into, and entitled to all the advantages of this union: but no other colony shall be admitted into the same, unless such admission be agreed to by nine states.

ARTICLE 12. All bills of credit emitted, monies borrowed, and debts contracted by or under the authority of congress, before the assembling of the united states, in pursuance of the present confederation, shall be deemed and considered as a charge against the united States, for payment and satisfaction whereof the said united states and the public faith are hereby solemnly pledged.

ARTICLE 13. Every State shall abide by the determinations of the united states, in congress assembled, on all questions which by this confederation are submitted to them. And the Articles of this confederation shall be inviolably observed by every state, and the union shall be perpetual; nor shall any alteration at any time hereafter be made in any of them, unless such alteration be agreed to in a congress of the united states, and be afterwards confirmed by the legislatures of every state.

And Whereas it hath pleased the Great Governor of the World to incline the hearts of the legislatures we respectively represent in congress, to approve of, and to authorize us to ratify the said articles of confederation and perpetual union, Know Ye, that we, the undersigned delegates, by virtue of the power and authority to us given for that purpose, do, by these presents, in the name and in behalf of our respective constituents, fully and entirely ratify and confirm each and every of the said articles of confederation and perpetual union, and all and singular the matters and things therein contained. And we do further solemnly plight and engage the faith of our respective constituents, that they shall abide by the determinations of the united states in congress assembled, on all questions, which by the said confederation are submitted to them. And that the articles thereof shall be inviolably observed by the states we respectively represent, and that the union shall be perpetual.

BATTLE OF BUNKER HILL.

In Witness whereof, we have hereunto set our hands, in Congress. Done at Philadelphia, in the State of Pennsylvania, the ninth Day of July, in the Year of our Lord one Thousand seven Hundred and Seventy eight, and in the third year of the Independence of America.[9]

NEW HAMPSHIRE
Josiah Bartlett,
John Wentworth, jun.

MASSACHUSETTS BAY
John Hancock,
Samuel Adams,
Elbridge Gerry,
Francis Dana,
James Lovell,
Samuel Holten.

RHODE ISLAND
William Ellery,
Henry Marchant,
John Collins.

CONNECTICUT
Roger Sherman,
Samuel Huntington,
Oliver Wolcott,
Titus Hosmer,
Andrew Adams.

NEW YORK
Jas. Duane,
Fra. Lewis,
Wm. Duer,
Gouv. Morris.

NEW JERSEY
Jno. Witherspoon,
Nath. Scudder.

PENNSYLVANIA
Robt. Morris,
Daniel Roberdeau,
Jona. Bayard Smith,
William Clingan,
Joseph Reed.

DELAWARE
Thos. M'Kean,
John Dickinson,
Nicholas Van Dyke.

MARYLAND
John Hanson,
Daniel Carroll.

VIRGINIA
Richard Henry Lee,
John Bannister,
Thomas Adams,
Jno. Harvie,
Francis Lightfoot Lee.

NORTH CAROLINA
John Penn,
Cons. Harnett,
Jno. Williams.

SOUTH CAROLINA
Henry Laurens,
William Henry Drayton,
Jno. Matthews,
Richard Hutson,
Thos. Heyward, jun.

GEORGIA
Jno. Walton,
Edwd. Telfair,
Edwd. Langworthy.

THE BOSTON TEA PARTY.

WASHINGTON SENDING HIS ULTIMATUM TO CORNWALLIS.

AMERICA'S SECOND CONSTITUTION

Constitution of the United States of America

ORIGINAL FIRST PAGE OF THE CONSTITUTION OF THE UNITED STATES OF AMERICA.

Constitution of the United States of America

- The U.S. Constitution was created in response to what Liberals at the time viewed as "weaknesses" in the Articles of Confederation. In essence, they believed that the Articles gave too much power to the states and not enough to the central or national government. Conservatives, however, intentionally created the Articles this way and saw no reason to alter them.
- Due to increasing Left-wing dissatisfaction over our first constitution (a faction greatly motivated by Liberal Alexander Hamilton), in May 1786, Charles Pinckney of South Carolina suggested revising the Articles. To this end the Continental Congress appointed a committee to begin drafting additional amendments, which it completed on August 7, 1786.
- Intense debate over the Articles continued into 1787. With agreement between Conservatives and Liberals impossible, a decision was made to replace the Articles entirely with a new document, one to be called the Constitution of the United States of America. The revised amendments to the Articles were discarded, and Edmund Randolph, James Wilson, Oliver Ellsworth, as well as several others, began writing up a number of drafts. George Washington, James Madison, and Rufus King also contributed. These drafts were fiercely contended at the Philadelphia Convention, which was held from May 14, 1787, to September 17, 1787. On the latter date the new constitution was adopted.
- On March 4, 1789, the U.S. Constitution officially replaced the Articles of Confederation. On June 21, 1789, the U.S. Constitution was fully ratified (by nine states), becoming our second constitution.
- In overturning and replacing the Articles a new form of government was created, one designed around the concept of the separation of powers into three branches: the executive, the judiciary, and the legislative.
- The U.S. Constitution greatly weakened the state governments while greatly strengthening the national government—which is why Thomas Paine, Patrick Henry, and many other Conservatives bitterly opposed it.

Life Span of the U.S. Constitution: 1789-Present

PHILADELPHIA, PENNSYLVANIA, CIRCA 1775.

W E THE PEOPLE OF THE United States, in Order to form a more perfect Union, establish Justice, insure domestic Tranquility, provide for the common defence, promote the general Welfare, and secure the Blessings of Liberty to ourselves and our Posterity, do ordain and establish this Constitution for the United States of America.

ARTICLE 1

Section 1: Congress
All legislative Powers herein granted shall be vested in a Congress of the United States, which shall consist of a Senate and House of Representatives.

Section 2: The House of Representatives
The House of Representatives shall be composed of Members chosen every second Year by the People of the several States, and the Electors in each State shall have the Qualifications requisite for Electors of the most numerous Branch of the State Legislature.

No Person shall be a Representative who shall not have attained to the Age of twenty five Years, and been seven Years a Citizen of the United States, and who shall not, when elected, be an Inhabitant of that State in which he shall be chosen.

PATRICK HENRY.

Representatives and direct Taxes shall be apportioned among the several States which may be included within this Union, according to their respective Numbers, which shall be determined by adding to the whole Number of free Persons, including those bound to Service for a Term of Years, and excluding Indians not taxed, three fifths of all other Persons. The actual Enumeration shall be made within three Years after the first Meeting of the Congress of the United States, and within every subsequent Term of ten Years, in such Manner as they shall by Law direct. The number of Representatives shall not exceed one for every thirty Thousand, but each State shall have at Least one Representative; and until such enumeration shall be made, the State of New Hampshire shall be entitled to chuse three, Massachusetts eight, Rhode-Island and Providence Plantations one, Connecticut five, New-York six, New Jersey four, Pennsylvania eight, Delaware one, Maryland six, Virginia ten, North Carolina five, South Carolina five, and Georgia three.

When vacancies happen in the Representation from any State, the Executive Authority thereof shall issue Writs of Election to fill such Vacancies.

The House of Representatives shall chuse their Speaker and other Officers; and shall have the sole Power of Impeachment.

Section 3: The Senate
The Senate of the United States shall be composed of two Senators from each State, chosen by the Legislature thereof, for six Years; and each Senator shall have one Vote.

Immediately after they shall be assembled in Consequence of the first Election, they shall be divided as equally as may be into three Classes. The Seats of the Senators of the first Class shall be vacated at the Expiration of the second Year, of the second Class at the Expiration of the fourth Year, and of the third Class at the Expiration of the sixth Year, so that one third may be chosen every second Year; and if Vacancies happen by Resignation, or otherwise, during the Recess of the Legislature of any State, the Executive thereof may make temporary Appointments until the next Meeting of the Legislature, which shall then fill such Vacancies.

GEORGE WASHINGTON, COMMANDER OF ALL CONTINENTAL ARMIES, AND FIRST PRESIDENT OF THE U.S.A. UNDER THE U.S. CONSTITUTION.

No Person shall be a Senator who shall not have attained to the Age of thirty Years, and been nine Years a Citizen of the United States, and who shall not, when elected, be an Inhabitant of that State for which he shall be chosen.

The Vice President of the United States shall be President of the Senate, but shall have no Vote, unless they be equally divided.

The Senate shall chuse their other Officers, and also a President pro tempore, in the Absence of the Vice President, or when he shall exercise the Office of President of the United States.

The Senate shall have the sole Power to try all Impeachments. When sitting for that Purpose, they shall be on Oath or Affirmation. When the

President of the United States is tried, the Chief Justice shall preside: And no Person shall be convicted without the Concurrence of two thirds of the Members present.

Judgment in Cases of Impeachment shall not extend further than to removal from Office, and disqualification to hold and enjoy any Office of honor, Trust or Profit under the United States: but the Party convicted shall nevertheless be liable and subject to Indictment, Trial, Judgment and Punishment, according to Law.

Section 4: Elections
The Times, Places and Manner of holding Elections for Senators and Representatives, shall be prescribed in each State by the Legislature thereof; but the Congress may at any time by Law make or alter such Regulations, except as to the Places of chusing Senators.

The Congress shall assemble at least once in every Year, and such Meeting shall be on the first Monday in December, unless they shall by Law appoint a different Day.

Section 5: Powers and Duties of Congress
Each House shall be the Judge of the Elections, Returns and Qualifications of its own Members, and a Majority of each shall constitute a Quorum to do Business; but a smaller Number may adjourn from day to day, and may be authorized to compel the Attendance of absent Members, in such Manner, and under such Penalties as each House may provide.

Each House may determine the Rules of its Proceedings, punish its Members for disorderly Behaviour, and, with the Concurrence of two thirds, expel a Member.

Each House shall keep a Journal of its Proceedings, and from time to time publish the same, excepting such Parts as may in their Judgment require Secrecy; and the Yeas and Nays of the Members of either House on any question shall, at the Desire of one fifth of those Present, be entered on the Journal.

Neither House, during the Session of Congress, shall, without the Consent of the other, adjourn for more than three days, nor to any other Place than that in which the two Houses shall be sitting.

Section 6: Rights and Disabilities of Members
The Senators and Representatives shall receive a Compensation for their Services, to be ascertained by Law, and paid out of the Treasury of the United States. They shall in all Cases, except Treason, Felony and Breach

of the Peace, be privileged from Arrest during their Attendance at the Session of their respective Houses, and in going to and returning from the same; and for any Speech or Debate in either House, they shall not be questioned in any other Place.

No Senator or Representative shall, during the Time for which he was elected, be appointed to any civil Office under the Authority of the United States, which shall have been created, or the Emoluments whereof shall have been increased during such time; and no Person holding any Office under the United States, shall be a Member of either House during his Continuance in Office.

Section 7: Legislative Process
All Bills for raising Revenue shall originate in the House of Representatives; but the Senate may propose or concur with Amendments as on other Bills.

Every Bill which shall have passed the House of Representatives and the Senate, shall, before it become a Law, be presented to the President of the United States; If he approve he shall sign it, but if not he shall return it, with his Objections to that House in which it shall have originated, who shall enter the Objections at large on their Journal, and proceed to reconsider it. If after such Reconsideration two thirds of that House shall agree to pass the Bill, it shall be sent, together with the Objections, to the other House, by which it shall likewise be reconsidered, and if approved by two thirds of that House, it shall become a Law. But in all such Cases the Votes of both Houses shall be determined by Yeas and Nays, and the Names of the Persons voting for and against the Bill shall be entered on the Journal of each House respectively. If any Bill shall not be returned by the President within ten Days (Sundays excepted) after it shall have been presented to him, the Same shall be a Law, in like Manner as if he had signed it, unless the Congress by their Adjournment prevent its Return, in which Case it shall not be a Law.

Every Order, Resolution, or Vote to which the Concurrence of the Senate and House of Representatives may be necessary (except on a question of Adjournment) shall be presented to the President of the United States; and before the Same

THE BATTLE OF LEXINGTON.

shall take Effect, shall be approved by him, or being disapproved by him, shall be repassed by two thirds of the Senate and House of Representatives, according to the Rules and Limitations prescribed in the Case of a Bill.

Section 8: Powers of Congress
The Congress shall have Power To lay and collect Taxes, Duties, Imposts and Excises, to pay the Debts and provide for the common Defence and general Welfare of the United States; but all Duties, Imposts and Excises shall be uniform throughout the United States;

To borrow Money on the credit of the United States;

To regulate Commerce with foreign Nations, and among the several States, and with the Indian Tribes;

To establish a uniform Rule of Naturalization, and uniform Laws on the subject of Bankruptcies throughout the United States;

To coin Money, regulate the Value thereof, and of foreign Coin, and fix the Standard of Weights and Measures;

To provide for the Punishment of counterfeiting the Securities and current Coin of the United States;

To establish Post Offices and post Roads;

To promote the Progress of Science and useful Arts, by securing for limited Times to Authors and Inventors the exclusive Right to their respective Writings and Discoveries;

To constitute Tribunals inferior to the supreme Court;

To define and punish Piracies and Felonies committed on the high Seas, and Offenses against the Law of Nations;

To declare War, grant Letters of Marque and Reprisal, and make Rules concerning Captures on Land and Water;

To raise and support Armies, but no Appropriation of Money to that Use shall be for a longer Term than two Years;

To provide and maintain a Navy;

To make Rules for the Government and Regulation of the land and naval Forces;

To provide for calling forth the Militia to execute the Laws of the Union, suppress Insurrections and repel Invasions;

To provide for organizing, arming, and disciplining, the Militia, and for governing such Part of them as may be employed in the Service of the United States, reserving to the States respectively, the Appointment of the Officers, and the Authority of training the Militia according to the discipline prescribed by Congress;

RETREAT FROM CONCORD.

To exercise exclusive Legislation in all Cases whatsoever, over such District (not exceeding ten Miles square) as may, by Cession of particular States, and the Acceptance of Congress, become the Seat of the Government of the United States, and to exercise like Authority over all Places purchased by the Consent of the Legislature of the State in which the Same shall be, for the Erection of Forts, Magazines, Arsenals, dock-Yards and other needful Buildings;—And

To make all Laws which shall be necessary and proper for carrying into Execution the foregoing Powers, and all other Powers vested by this Constitution in the Government of the United States, or in any Department or Officer thereof.

Section 9: Powers Denied Congress
The Migration or Importation of such Persons as any of the States now existing shall think proper to admit, shall not be prohibited by the Congress prior to the Year one thousand eight hundred and eight, but a Tax or duty may be imposed on such Importation, not exceeding ten dollars for each Person.

The Privilege of the Writ of Habeas Corpus shall not be suspended, unless when in Cases of Rebellion or Invasion the public Safety may require it.

No Bill of Attainder or ex post facto Law shall be passed.

No Capitation, or other direct, Tax shall be laid, unless in Proportion to the Census or Enumeration herein before directed to be taken.

No Tax or Duty shall be laid on Articles exported from any State.

No Preference shall be given by any Regulation of Commerce or Revenue to the Ports of one State over those of another: nor shall Vessels bound to, or from, one State, be obliged to enter, clear, or pay Duties in another.

No Money shall be drawn from the Treasury, but in Consequence of Appropriations made by Law; and a regular Statement and Account of the Receipts and Expenditures of all public Money shall be published from time to time.

No Title of Nobility shall be granted by the United States: And no Person holding any Office of Profit or Trust under them, shall, without the Consent of the Congress, accept of any present, Emolument, Office, or Title, of any kind whatever, from any King, Prince, or foreign State.

Section 10: Powers Denied to the States
No State shall enter into any Treaty, Alliance, or Confederation; grant Letters of Marque and Reprisal; coin Money; emit Bills of Credit; make any Thing but gold and silver Coin a Tender in Payment of Debts; pass any Bill of Attainder, ex post facto Law, or Law impairing the Obligation of Contracts, or grant any Title of Nobility.

No State shall, without the Consent of the Congress, lay any Imposts or Duties on Imports or Exports, except what may be absolutely necessary for executing it's inspection Laws: and the net Produce of all Duties and Imposts, laid by any State on Imports or Exports, shall be for the Use of the Treasury of the United States; and all such Laws shall be subject to the Revision and Controul of the Congress.

No State shall, without the Consent of Congress, lay any Duty of Tonnage, keep Troops, or Ships of War in time of Peace, enter into any Agreement or Compact with another State, or with a foreign Power, or engage in War, unless actually invaded, or in such imminent Danger as will not admit of delay.

ARTICLE 2
Section 1
The executive Power shall be vested in a President of the United States of America. He shall hold his Office during the Term of four Years, and, together with the Vice President, chosen for the same Term, be elected, as follows:

Each State shall appoint, in such Manner as the Legislature thereof may direct, a Number of Electors, equal to the whole Number of Senators and Representatives to which the State may be entitled in the Congress: but no Senator or Representative, or Person holding an Office of Trust or Profit under the United States, shall be appointed an Elector.

The Electors shall meet in their respective States, and vote by Ballot for two Persons, of whom one at least shall not be an Inhabitant of the same State with themselves. And they shall make a List of all the Persons voted for, and of the Number of Votes for each; which List they shall sign and certify, and transmit sealed to the Seat of the Government of the United States, directed to the President of the Senate. The President of the Senate shall, in the Presence of the Senate and House of Representatives, open all the Certificates, and the Votes shall then be counted. The Person having the greatest Number of Votes shall be the President, if such Number be a Majority of the whole Number of Electors appointed; and if there be more than one who have such Majority, and have an equal Number of Votes, then the House of Representatives shall immediately chuse by Ballot one of them for President; and if no Person have a Majority, then from the five highest on the List the said House shall in like Manner chuse the President. But in chusing the President, the Votes

BARON FRIEDRICH VON STEUBEN, GENERAL IN THE CONTINENTAL ARMY AND ADVISER TO WASHINGTON.

shall be taken by States, the Representation from each State having one Vote; A quorum for this Purpose shall consist of a Member or Members from two thirds of the States, and a Majority of all the States shall be necessary to a Choice. In every Case, after the Choice of the President, the Person having the greatest Number of Votes of the Electors shall be the Vice President. But if there should remain two or more who have equal Votes, the Senate shall chuse from them by Ballot the Vice President.

The Congress may determine the Time of chusing the Electors, and the Day on which they shall give their Votes; which Day shall be the same throughout the United States.

No Person except a natural born Citizen, or a Citizen of the United States, at the time of the Adoption of this Constitution, shall be eligible to the Office of President; neither shall any person be eligible to that Office who shall not have attained to the Age of thirty five Years, and been fourteen Years a Resident within the United States.

In Case of the Removal of the President from Office, or of his Death, Resignation, or Inability to discharge the Powers and Duties of the said Office, the Same shall devolve on the Vice President, and the Congress may by Law provide for the Case of Removal, Death, Resignation or Inability, both of the President and Vice President, declaring what Officer shall then act as President, and such Officer shall act accordingly, until the Disability be removed, or a President shall be elected.

The President shall, at stated Times, receive for his Services, a Compensation, which shall neither be increased nor diminished during the Period for which he shall have been elected, and he shall not receive within that Period any other Emolument from the United States, or any of them.

Before he enter on the Execution of his Office, he shall take the following Oath or Affirmation:—"I do solemnly swear (or affirm) that I will faithfully execute the Office of President of the United States, and will to the best of my Ability, preserve, protect and defend the Constitution of the United States."

Section 2
The President shall be Commander in Chief of the Army and Navy of the United States, and of the Militia of the several States, when called into the actual Service of the United States; he may require the Opinion, in writing, of the principal Officer in each of the executive Departments, upon any Subject relating to the Duties of their respective Offices, and he shall have Power to grant Reprieves and Pardons for Offenses against the United States, except in Cases of Impeachment.

He shall have Power, by and with the Advice and Consent of the Senate, to make Treaties, provided two thirds of the Senators present concur; and he shall nominate, and by and with the Advice and Consent of the Senate, shall appoint Ambassadors, other public Ministers and Consuls, Judges of the supreme Court, and all other Officers of the United States, whose Appointments are not herein otherwise provided for, and which shall be established by Law: but the Congress may by Law vest the

Appointment of such inferior Officers, as they think proper, in the President alone, in the Courts of Law, or in the Heads of Departments.

The President shall have Power to fill up all Vacancies that may happen during the Recess of the Senate, by granting Commissions which shall expire at the End of their next Session.

Section 3
He shall from time to time give to the Congress Information of the State of the Union, and recommend to their Consideration such Measures as he shall judge necessary and expedient; he may, on extraordinary Occasions, convene both Houses, or either of them, and in Case of Disagreement between them, with Respect to the Time of Adjournment, he may adjourn them to such Time as he shall think proper; he shall receive Ambassadors and other public Ministers; he shall take Care that the Laws be faithfully executed, and shall Commission all the Officers of the United States.

BATTLE OF PRINCETON.

Section 4
The President, Vice President and all civil Officers of the United States, shall be removed from Office on Impeachment for, and Conviction of, Treason, Bribery, or other high Crimes and Misdemeanors.

ARTICLE 3
Section 1
The judicial Power of the United States, shall be vested in one supreme Court, and in such inferior Courts as the Congress may from time to

time ordain and establish. The Judges, both of the supreme and inferior Courts, shall hold their Offices during good Behaviour, and shall, at stated Times, receive for their Services, a Compensation, which shall not be diminished during their Continuance in Office.

Section 2

The judicial Power shall extend to all Cases, in Law and Equity, arising under this Constitution, the Laws of the United States, and Treaties made, or which shall be made, under their Authority;—to all Cases affecting Ambassadors, other public Ministers and Consuls;—to all Cases of admiralty and maritime Jurisdiction;—to Controversies to which the United States shall be a Party;—to Controversies between two or more States;—between a State and Citizens of another State;—between Citizens of different States;—between Citizens of the same State claiming Lands under Grants of different States, and between a State, or the Citizens thereof, and foreign States, Citizens or Subjects.

In all Cases affecting Ambassadors, other public Ministers and Consuls, and those in which a State shall be Party, the supreme Court shall have original Jurisdiction. In all the other Cases before mentioned, the supreme Court shall have appellate Jurisdiction, both as to Law and Fact, with such Exceptions, and under such Regulations as the Congress shall make.

The Trial of all Crimes, except in Cases of Impeachment; shall be by Jury; and such Trial shall be held in the State where the said Crimes shall have been committed; but when not committed within any State, the Trial shall be at such Place or Places as the Congress may by Law have directed.

Section 3

Treason against the United States, shall consist only in levying War against them, or in adhering to their Enemies, giving them Aid and Comfort. No Person shall be convicted of Treason unless on the Testimony of two Witnesses to the same overt Act, or on Confession in open Court.

The Congress shall have Power to declare the Punishment of Treason, but no Attainder of Treason shall work Corruption of Blood, or Forfeiture except during the Life of the Person attainted.

ARTICLE 4

Section 1

Full Faith and Credit shall be given in each State to the public Acts, Records, and judicial Proceedings of every other State. And the Congress may by general Laws prescribe the Manner in which such Acts, Records and Proceedings shall be proved, and the Effect thereof.

Section 2
The Citizens of each State shall be entitled to all Privileges and Immunities of Citizens in the several States.

A Person charged in any State with Treason, Felony, or other Crime, who shall flee from Justice, and be found in another State, shall on Demand of the executive Authority of the State from which he fled, be delivered up, to be removed to the State having Jurisdiction of the Crime.

No Person held to Service or Labour in one State, under the Laws thereof, escaping into another, shall, in Consequence of any Law or Regulation therein, be discharged from such Service or Labour, but shall be delivered up on Claim of the Party to whom such Service or Labour may be due.

Section 3
New States may be admitted by the Congress into this Union; but no new State shall be formed or erected within the Jurisdiction of any other State; nor any State be formed by the Junction of two or more States, or Parts of States, without the Consent of the Legislatures of the States concerned as well as of the Congress.

The Congress shall have Power to dispose of and make all needful Rules and Regulations respecting the Territory or other Property belonging to the United States; and nothing in this Constitution shall be so construed as to Prejudice any Claims of the United States, or of any particular State.

AMERICAN REVOLUTIONARY WAR GENERAL NATHANAEL GREENE.

Section 4
The United States shall guarantee to every State in this Union a Republican Form of Government, and shall protect each of them against Invasion; and on Application of the Legislature, or of the Executive (when the Legislature cannot be convened) against domestic Violence.

ARTICLE 5

The Congress, whenever two thirds of both Houses shall deem it necessary, shall propose Amendments to this Constitution, or, on the Application of the Legislatures of two thirds of the several States, shall call a Convention for proposing Amendments, which, in either Case, shall be valid to all Intents and Purposes, as Part of this Constitution, when ratified by the Legislatures of three fourths of the several States, or by Conventions in three fourths thereof, as the one or the other Mode of Ratification may be proposed by the Congress; Provided that no Amendment which may be made prior to the Year One thousand eight hundred and eight shall in any Manner affect the first and fourth Clauses in the Ninth Section of the first Article; and that no State, without its Consent, shall be deprived of its equal Suffrage in the Senate.

ARTICLE 6

All Debts contracted and Engagements entered into, before the Adoption of this Constitution, shall be as valid against the United States under this Constitution, as under the Confederation.

This Constitution, and the Laws of the United States which shall be made in Pursuance thereof; and all Treaties made, or which shall be made, under the Authority of the United States, shall be the supreme Law of the Land; and the Judges in every State shall be bound thereby, any Thing in the Constitution or Laws of any State to the Contrary notwithstanding.

The Senators and Representatives before mentioned, and the Members of the several State Legislatures, and all executive and judicial Officers, both of the United States and of the several States, shall be bound by Oath or Affirmation, to support this Constitution; but no religious Test shall ever be required as a Qualification to any Office or public Trust under the United States.

ARTICLE 7

The Ratification of the Conventions of nine States, shall be sufficient for the Establishment of this Constitution between the States so ratifying the Same.

1st Amendment (1791)
Congress shall make no law respecting an establishment of religion, or prohibiting the free exercise thereof; or abridging the freedom of speech, or of the press; or the right of the people peaceably to assemble, and to petition the Government for a redress of grievances.

2nd Amendment (1791)
A well regulated Militia, being necessary to the security of a free State,

the right of the people to keep and bear Arms, shall not be infringed.

3rd Amendment (1791)
No Soldier shall, in time of peace be quartered in any house, without the consent of the Owner, nor in time of war, but in a manner to be prescribed by law.

4th Amendment (1791)
The right of the people to be secure in their persons, houses, papers, and effects, against unreasonable searches and seizures, shall not be violated, and no Warrants shall issue, but upon probable cause, supported by Oath or affirmation, and particularly describing the place to be searched, and the persons or things to be seized.

BATTLE OF THE COWPENS.

5th Amendment (1791)
No person shall be held to answer for a capital, or otherwise infamous crime, unless on a presentment or indictment of a Grand Jury, except in cases arising in the land or naval forces, or in the Militia, when in actual service in time of War or public danger; nor shall any person be subject for the same offence to be twice put in jeopardy of life or limb; nor shall be compelled in any criminal case to be a witness against himself, nor be deprived of life, liberty, or property, without due process of law; nor shall private property be taken for public use, without just compensation.

6th Amendment (1791)
In all criminal prosecutions, the accused shall enjoy the right to a speedy and public trial, by an impartial jury of the State and district wherein the crime shall have been committed, which district shall have been previously ascertained by law, and to be informed of the nature and cause of the accusation; to be confronted with the witnesses against him; to have compulsory process for obtaining witnesses in his favor, and to have the Assistance of Counsel for his defence.

7th Amendment (1791)
In Suits at common law, where the value in controversy shall exceed twenty dollars, the right of trial by jury shall be preserved, and no fact tried by a jury, shall be otherwise reexamined in any Court of the United States, than according to the rules of the common law.

8th Amendment (1791)
Excessive bail shall not be required, nor excessive fines imposed, nor cruel and unusual punishments inflicted.

9th Amendment (1791)
The enumeration in the Constitution, of certain rights, shall not be construed to deny or disparage others retained by the people.

10th Amendment (1791)
The powers not delegated to the United States by the Constitution, nor prohibited by it to the States, are reserved to the States respectively, or to the people.

11th Amendment (1798)
The Judicial power of the United States shall not be construed to extend to any suit in law or equity, commenced or prosecuted against one of the United States by Citizens of another State, or by Citizens or Subjects of any Foreign State.

12th Amendment (1804)
The Electors shall meet in their respective states and vote by ballot for President and Vice-President, one of whom, at least, shall not be an inhabitant of the same state with themselves; they shall name in their ballots the person voted for as President, and in distinct ballots the person voted for as Vice-President, and they shall make distinct lists of all persons voted for as President, and of all persons voted for as Vice-President, and of the number of votes for each, which lists they shall sign and certify, and transmit sealed to the seat of the government of the United States, directed to the President of the Senate;—The President of the Senate shall, in the presence of the Senate and House of Representatives, open all the certificates and the votes shall then be

AMERICAN REVOLUTIONARY WAR COMMANDER HENRY "LIGHT-HORSE HARRY" LEE; FATHER OF CONFEDERATE GENERAL ROBERT E. LEE.

counted;—The person having the greatest number of votes for President, shall be the President, if such number be a majority of the whole number of Electors appointed; and if no person have such majority, then from the persons having the highest numbers not exceeding three on the list of those voted for as President, the House of Representatives shall choose immediately, by ballot, the President. But in choosing the President, the votes shall be taken by states, the representation from each state having one vote; a quorum for this purpose shall consist of a member or members from two-thirds of the states, and a majority of all the states shall be necessary to a choice. And if the House of Representatives shall not choose a President whenever the right of choice shall devolve upon them, before the fourth day of March next following, then the Vice-President shall act as President, as in case of the death or other constitutional disability of the President.—The person having the greatest number of votes as Vice-President, shall be the Vice-President, if such number be a majority of the whole number of Electors appointed, and if no person have a majority, then from the two highest numbers on the list, the Senate shall choose the Vice-President; a quorum for the purpose shall consist of two-thirds of the whole number of Senators, and a majority of the whole number shall be necessary to a choice. But no person constitutionally ineligible to the office of President shall be eligible to that of Vice-President of the United States.

13ᵗʰ Amendment (1865)
Section 1
Neither slavery nor involuntary servitude, except as a punishment for crime whereof the party shall have been duly convicted, shall exist within the United States, or any place subject to their jurisdiction.

Section 2
Congress shall have power to enforce this article by appropriate legislation.

14ᵗʰ Amendment (1868)
Section 1
All persons born or naturalized in the United States, and subject to the

jurisdiction thereof, are citizens of the United States and of the State wherein they reside. No State shall make or enforce any law which shall abridge the privileges or immunities of citizens of the United States; nor shall any State deprive any person of life, liberty, or property, without due process of law; nor deny to any person within its jurisdiction the equal protection of the laws.

Section 2
Representatives shall be apportioned among the several States according to their respective numbers, counting the whole number of persons in each State, excluding Indians not taxed. But when the right to vote at any election for the choice of electors for President and Vice-President of the United States, Representatives in Congress, the Executive and Judicial officers of a State, or the members of the Legislature thereof, is denied to any of the male inhabitants of such State, being twenty-one years of age, and citizens of the United States, or in any way abridged, except for participation in rebellion, or other crime, the basis of representation therein shall be reduced in the proportion which the number of such male citizens shall bear to the whole number of male citizens twenty-one years of age in such State.

Section 3
No person shall be a Senator or Representative in Congress, or elector of President and Vice-President, or hold any office, civil or military, under the United States, or under any State, who, having previously taken an oath, as a member of Congress, or as an officer of the United States, or as a member of any State legislature, or as an executive or judicial officer of any State, to support the Constitution of the United States, shall have engaged in insurrection or rebellion against the same, or given aid or comfort to the enemies thereof. But Congress may by a vote of two-thirds of each House, remove such disability.

Section 4
The validity of the public debt of the United States, authorized by law, including debts incurred for payment of pensions and bounties for services in suppressing insurrection or rebellion, shall not be questioned. But neither the United States nor any State shall assume or pay any debt or obligation incurred in aid of insurrection or rebellion against the United States, or any claim for the loss or emancipation of any slave; but all such debts, obligations and claims shall be held illegal and void.

Section 5
The Congress shall have the power to enforce, by appropriate legislation, the provisions of this article.

15th Amendment (1870)
Section 1
The right of citizens of the United States to vote shall not be denied or abridged by the United States or by any State on account of race, color, or previous condition of servitude.

Section 2
The Congress shall have the power to enforce this article by appropriate legislation.

16th Amendment (1913)
The Congress shall have power to lay and collect taxes on incomes, from whatever source derived, without apportionment among the several States, and without regard to any census or enumeration.

17th Amendment (1913)
The Senate of the United States shall be composed of two Senators from each State, elected by the people thereof, for six years; and each Senator shall have one vote. The electors in each State shall have the qualifications requisite for electors of the most numerous branch of the State legislatures.

When vacancies happen in the representation of any State in the Senate, the executive authority of such State shall issue writs of election to fill such vacancies: Provided, That the legislature of any State may empower the executive thereof to make temporary appointments until the people fill the vacancies by election as the legislature may direct.

This amendment shall not be so construed as to affect the election or term of any Senator chosen before it becomes valid as part of the Constitution.

MOLLY PITCHER AT THE BATTLE OF MONMOUTH.

18th Amendment (1919)
Section 1
After one year from the ratification of this article the manufacture, sale, or transportation of intoxicating liquors within, the importation thereof into, or the exportation thereof from the United States and all territory subject to the jurisdiction thereof for beverage purposes is hereby prohibited.

Section 2
The Congress and the several States shall have concurrent power to enforce this article by appropriate legislation.

Section 3
This article shall be inoperative unless it shall have been ratified as an amendment to the Constitution by the legislatures of the several States, as provided in the Constitution, within seven years from the date of the submission hereof to the States by the Congress.

19th Amendment (1920)
The right of citizens of the United States to vote shall not be denied or abridged by the United States or by any State on account of sex.

Congress shall have power to enforce this article by appropriate legislation.

20th Amendment (1933)
Section 1
The terms of the President and the Vice President shall end at noon on the 20th day of January, and the terms of Senators and Representatives at noon on the 3rd day of January, of the years in which such terms would have ended if this article had not been ratified; and the terms of their successors shall then begin.

Section 2
The Congress shall assemble at least once in every year, and such meeting shall begin at noon on the 3rd day of January, unless they shall by law appoint a different day.

Section 3
If, at the time fixed for the beginning of the term of the President, the President elect shall have died, the Vice President elect shall become President. If a President shall not have been chosen before the time fixed for the beginning of his term, or if the President elect shall have failed to qualify, then the Vice President elect shall act as President until a President shall have qualified; and the Congress may by law provide for the case wherein neither a President elect nor a Vice President shall have

qualified, declaring who shall then act as President, or the manner in which one who is to act shall be selected, and such person shall act accordingly until a President or Vice President shall have qualified.

Section 4
The Congress may by law provide for the case of the death of any of the persons from whom the House of Representatives may choose a President whenever the right of choice shall have devolved upon them, and for the case of the death of any of the persons from whom the Senate may choose a Vice President whenever the right of choice shall have devolved upon them.

Section 5
Sections 1 and 2 shall take effect on the 15th day of October following the ratification of this article.

Section 6
This article shall be inoperative unless it shall have been ratified as an amendment to the Constitution by the legislatures of three-fourths of the several States within seven years from the date of its submission.

21st Amendment (1933)
Section 1
The eighteenth article of amendment to the Constitution of the United States is hereby repealed.

Section 2
The transportation or importation into any State, Territory, or Possession of the United States for delivery or use therein of intoxicating liquors, in violation of the laws thereof, is hereby prohibited.

Section 3
This article shall be inoperative unless it shall have been ratified as an amendment to the Constitution by conventions in the several States, as provided in the Constitution, within seven years from the date of the submission hereof to the States by the Congress.

22nd Amendment (1951)
Section 1
No person shall be elected to the office of the President more than

SAMUEL ADAMS.

twice, and no person who has held the office of President, or acted as President, for more than two years of a term to which some other person was elected President shall be elected to the office of President more than once. But this Article shall not apply to any person holding the office of President when this Article was proposed by Congress, and shall not prevent any person who may be holding the office of President, or acting as President, during the term within which this Article becomes operative from holding the office of President or acting as President during the remainder of such term.

Section 2
This article shall be inoperative unless it shall have been ratified as an amendment to the Constitution by the legislatures of three-fourths of the several States within seven years from the date of its submission to the States by the Congress.

23rd Amendment (1961)
Section 1
The District constituting the seat of Government of the United States shall appoint in such manner as Congress may direct:

A number of electors of President and Vice President equal to the whole number of Senators and Representatives in Congress to which the District would be entitled if it were a State, but in no event more than the least populous State; they shall be in addition to those appointed by the States, but they shall be considered, for the purposes of the election of President and Vice President, to be electors appointed by a State; and they shall meet in the District and perform such duties as provided by the twelfth article of amendment.

Section 2
The Congress shall have power to enforce this article by appropriate legislation.

24th Amendment (1964)
Section 1
The right of citizens of the United States to vote in any primary or other election for President or Vice President, for electors for President or Vice President, or for Senator or Representative in Congress, shall not be denied or abridged by the United States or any State by reason of failure to pay poll tax or other tax.

Section 2
The Congress shall have power to enforce this article by appropriate legislation.

25th Amendment (1967)
Section 1
In case of the removal of the President from office or of his death or resignation, the Vice President shall become President.

Section 2
Whenever there is a vacancy in the office of the Vice President, the President shall nominate a Vice President who shall take office upon confirmation by a majority vote of both Houses of Congress.

Section 3
Whenever the President transmits to the President pro tempore of the Senate and the Speaker of the House of Representatives his written declaration that he is unable to discharge the powers and duties of his office, and until he transmits to them a written declaration to the contrary, such powers and duties shall be discharged by the Vice President as Acting President.

WASHINGTON'S HEADQUARTERS AT CAMBRIDGE.

Section 4
Whenever the Vice President and a majority of either the principal officers of the executive departments or of such other body as Congress may by law provide, transmit to the President pro tempore of the Senate and the Speaker of the House of Representatives their written declaration that the President is unable to discharge the powers and duties of his office, the Vice President shall immediately assume the powers and duties of the office as Acting President.

Thereafter, when the President transmits to the President pro tempore of the Senate and the Speaker of the House of Representatives his written declaration that no inability exists, he shall resume the powers and duties of his office unless the Vice President and a majority of either the principal officers of the executive department or of such other body as Congress may by law provide, transmit within four days to the President pro tempore of the Senate and the Speaker of the House of Representatives their written declaration that the President is unable to discharge the powers and duties of his office. Thereupon Congress shall decide the issue, assembling within forty-eight hours for that purpose if not in session. If the Congress, within twenty-one days after receipt of the latter written declaration, or, if Congress is not in session, within twenty-one days after Congress is required to assemble, determines by two-thirds vote of both Houses that the President is unable to discharge the powers and duties of his office, the Vice President shall continue to discharge the same as Acting President; otherwise, the President shall resume the powers and duties of his office.

26th Amendment (1971)
Section 1
The right of citizens of the United States, who are eighteen years of age or older, to vote shall not be denied or abridged by the United States or by any State on account of age.

Section 2
The Congress shall have power to enforce this article by appropriate legislation.

27th Amendment (1992)
No law, varying the compensation for the services of the Senators and Representatives, shall take effect, until an election of representatives shall have intervened.

EVENING AFTER THE BATTLE OF TRENTON.

AMERICA'S THIRD CONSTITUTION

Constitution of the Confederate States of America

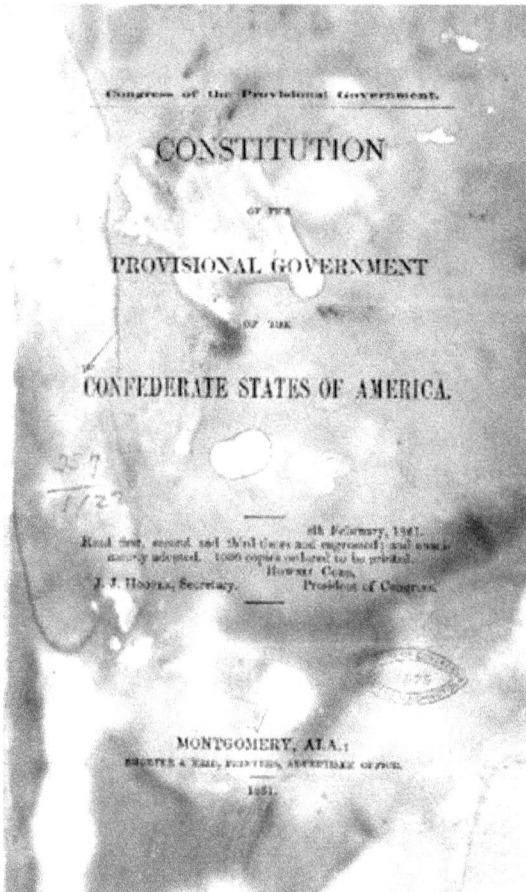

COVER PAGE OF THE CONSTITUTION OF THE CONFEDERATE
STATES OF AMERICA; PUBLISHED UNDER THE PROVISIONAL
CONFEDERATE CONGRESS AT MONTGOMERY, ALABAMA, 1861.

Constitution of the Confederate States of America

- The C.S. Constitution took some 35 days to write from start to finish, and was designed upon the Articles of Confederation and the U.S. Constitution.
- It was created to establish and form a new conservative republic: the Confederate States of America, which itself was intended to be a continuation of the government of the *original confederate republic*: the United States of America under confederation (1781-1789). The nickname of the original U.S. confederacy was borrowed by the seceding Southern states as well: The Confederate States of America—the C.S.A.
- The secession of the conservative Southern states was only necessary to begin with due to the man I refer to as America's 19th-Century King George III: Abraham Lincoln, a big government Liberal who had been implicitly threatening to disempower the states and enlarge the national government—then later, after becoming president, packed his administration and armies with socialists and communists as proof.
- The first draft of the C.S. Constitution began hurriedly on February 5, 1861, a mere four months after Lincoln's election.
- The writers were comprised of a 12-man committee headed by Christopher Memminger of South Carolina.
- The first draft was presented at the Montgomery Convention on February 7, 1861, and adopted on February 8, 1861. As this version was provisional, work continued on the final form.
- The final version of the C.S. Constitution was brought before the convention on February 28, 1861. Here it was unanimously adopted by the Confederate Congress on March 11, 1861, which represented the then seven states of the C.S.A.: South Carolina, Georgia, Florida, Alabama, Mississippi, Louisiana, and Texas. It was signed by 44 men from these seven states.
- Eventually, four more Southern states (Tennessee, Arkansas, North Carolina, and Virginia), and a portion of two additional Southern states (Kentucky and Missouri), would secede to become part of the Confederate States of America. The 13 stars on the C.S.A.'s national flags represent these 13 states—and symbolically the 13 colonies of the U.S.A. under confederation (1781-1789).
- Unlike the U.S. Constitution, the C.S. Constitution bans the slave trade (Article 1, Section 9, Clauses 1 and 2), further preparation for the day when complete abolition of slavery across the South was to be finalized. Note: In 1774 (Fairfax County Resolves) Southerners were already referring to slavery as a "wicked, cruel, and unnatural trade."

Life Span of the C.S. Constitution: 1861-Present
(Note: The C.S. government was never officially dissolved.)

PREAMBLE

W E, THE PEOPLE OF THE Confederate States, each State acting in its sovereign and independent character, in order to form a permanent federal government, establish justice, insure domestic tranquillity, and secure the blessings of liberty to ourselves and our posterity invoking the favor and guidance of Almighty God do ordain and establish this Constitution for the Confederate States of America.

ARTICLE 1

Section 1: All legislative powers herein delegated shall be vested in a Congress of the Confederate States, which shall consist of a Senate and House of Representatives.

INAUGURATION OF JEFFERSON DAVIS, PRESIDENT OF THE CONFEDERATE STATES OF AMERICA, AT MONTGOMERY, ALABAMA, FEBRUARY 18, 1861.

Section 2, Clause 1: The House of Representatives shall be composed of members chosen every second year by the people of the several States; and the electors in each State shall be citizens of the Confederate States, and have the qualifications requisite for electors of the most numerous branch of the State Legislature; but no person of foreign birth, not a citizen of the Confederate States, shall be allowed to vote for any officer, civil or political, State or Federal.

Section 2, Clause 2: No person shall be a Representative who shall not have attained the age of twenty-five years, and be a citizen of the Confederate States, and who shall not when elected, be an inhabitant of that State in which he shall be chosen.

Section 2, Clause 3: Representatives and direct taxes shall be apportioned among the several States, which may be included within this Confederacy, according to their respective numbers, which shall be determined by adding to the whole number of free persons, including those bound to service for a term of years, and excluding Indians not taxed, three-fifths of all slaves. The actual enumeration shall be made within three years after the first meeting of the Congress of the Confederate States, and within every subsequent term of ten years, in such manner as they shall by law direct. The number of Representatives shall not exceed one for every fifty thousand, but each State shall have at least one Representative; and until such enumeration shall be made, the State of South Carolina shall be entitled to choose

CONFEDERATE PRESIDENT JEFFERSON DAVIS.

six; the State of Georgia ten; the State of Alabama nine; the State of Florida two; the State of Mississippi seven; the State of Louisiana six; and the State of Texas six.

Section 2, Clause 4: When vacancies happen in the representation from any State the executive authority thereof shall issue writs of election to fill such vacancies.

Section 2, Clause 5: The House of Representatives shall choose their Speaker and other officers; and shall have the sole power of impeachment; except that any judicial or other Federal officer, resident and acting solely within the limits of any State, may be impeached by a vote of two-thirds of both branches of the Legislature thereof.

Section 3, Clause 1: The Senate of the Confederate States shall be composed of two Senators from each State, chosen for six years by the Legislature thereof, at the regular session next immediately preceding the commencement of the term of service; and each Senator shall have one vote.

Section 3, Clause 2: Immediately after they shall be assembled, in consequence of the first election, they shall be divided as equally as may be into three classes. The seats of the Senators of the first class shall be vacated at the expiration of the second year; of the second class at the expiration of the fourth year; and of the third class at the expiration of the sixth year; so that one-third may be chosen every second year; and if vacancies happen by resignation, or other wise, during the recess of the Legislature of any State, the Executive thereof may make temporary appointments until the next meeting of the Legislature, which shall then fill such vacancies.

Section 3, Clause 3: No person shall be a Senator who shall not have attained the age of thirty years, and be a citizen of the Confederate States; and who shall not, then elected, be an inhabitant of the State for which he shall be chosen.

Section 3, Clause 4: The Vice President of the Confederate States shall be president of the Senate, but shall have no vote unless they be equally divided.

Section 3, Clause 5: The Senate shall choose their other officers; and also a president pro tempore in the absence of the Vice President, or when he shall exercise the office of President of the Confederate states.

Section 3, Clause 6: The Senate shall have the sole power to try all impeachments. When sitting for that purpose, they shall be on oath or affirmation. When the President of the Confederate States is tried, the Chief Justice shall preside; and no person shall be convicted without the concurrence of two-thirds of the members present.

Section 3, Clause 7: Judgment in cases of impeachment shall not extend further than to removal from office, and disqualification to hold any office of honor, trust, or profit under the Confederate States; but the party convicted shall, nevertheless, be liable and subject to indictment, trial, judgment, and punishment according to law.

Section 4, Clause 1: The times, places, and manner of holding elections for Senators and Representatives shall be prescribed in each State by the Legislature thereof, subject to the provisions of this Constitution; but the Congress may, at any time, by law, make or alter such regulations, except as to the times and places of choosing Senators.

Section 4, Clause 2: The Congress shall assemble at least once in every year; and such meeting shall be on the first Monday in December, unless they shall, by law, appoint a different day.

Section 5, Clause 1: Each House shall be the judge of the elections, returns, and qualifications of its own members, and a majority of each shall constitute a quorum to do business; but a smaller number may adjourn from day to day, and may be authorized to compel the attendance of absent members, in such manner and under such penalties as each House may provide.

Section 5, Clause 2: Each House may determine the rules of its proceedings, punish its members for disorderly behavior, and, with the concurrence of two-thirds of the whole number, expel a member.

Section 5, Clause 3: Each House shall keep a journal of its proceedings, and from time to time publish the same, excepting such parts as may in their judgment require secrecy; and the yeas and nays of the members of either House, on any question, shall, at the desire of one-fifth of those present, be entered on the journal.

Section 5, Clause 4: Neither House, during the session of Congress, shall, without the consent of the other, adjourn for more than three days, nor to any other place than that in which the two Houses shall be sitting.

Section 6, Clause 1: The Senators and Representatives shall receive a compensation for their services, to be ascertained by law, and paid out of the Treasury of the Confederate States. They shall, in all cases, except treason, felony, and breach of the peace, be privileged from arrest during their attendance at the session of their respective Houses, and in going to and returning from the same; and for any speech or debate in either House, they shall not be questioned in any other place.

Section 6, Clause 2: No Senator or Representative shall, during the time for which he was elected, be appointed to any civil office under the authority of the Confederate States, which shall have been created, or the emoluments whereof shall have been increased during such time; and no

person holding any office under the Confederate States shall be a member of either House during his continuance in office. But Congress may, by law, grant to the principal officer in each of the Executive Departments a seat upon the floor of either House, with the privilege of discussing any measures appertaining to his department.

CONFEDERATE GENERAL JOHN BELL HOOD.

Section 7, Clause 1: All bills for raising revenue shall originate in the House of Representatives; but the Senate may propose or concur with amendments, as on other bills.

Section 7, Clause 2: Every bill which shall have passed both Houses, shall, before it becomes a law, be presented to the President of the Confederate States; if he approve, he shall sign it; but if not, he shall return it, with his objections, to that House in which it shall have originated, who shall enter the objections at large on their journal, and proceed to reconsider it. If, after such reconsideration, two-thirds of that House shall agree to pass the bill, it shall be sent, together with the objections, to the other House, by which it shall likewise be reconsidered, and if approved by two-thirds of that House, it shall become a law. But in all such cases, the votes of both Houses shall be determined by yeas and nays, and the names of the persons voting for and against the bill shall be entered on the journal of each House respectively. If any bill shall not be returned by the President within ten days (Sundays excepted) after it shall have been presented to him, the same shall be a law, in like manner as if he had signed it, unless the Congress, by their adjournment, prevent its return; in which case it shall not be a law. The President may approve any appropriation and disapprove any other appropriation in the same bill. In such case he shall, in signing the bill, designate the appropriations disapproved; and shall return a copy of such appropriations, with his objections, to the House in which the bill shall have originated; and the same proceedings shall then be had as in case of other bills disapproved by the President.

Section 7, Clause 3: Every order, resolution, or vote, to which the concurrence of both Houses may be necessary (except on a question of adjournment) shall be presented to the President of the Confederate States; and before the same shall take effect, shall be approved by him; or, being disapproved by him, shall be repassed by two-thirds of both Houses, according to the rules and limitations prescribed in case of a bill.

Section 8, Clause 1: The Congress shall have power to lay and collect taxes, duties, imposts, and excises for revenue, necessary to pay the debts, provide for the common defense, and carry on the Government of the Confederate States; but no bounties shall be granted from the Treasury; nor shall any duties or taxes on importations from foreign nations be laid to promote or foster any branch of industry; and all duties, imposts, and excises shall be uniform throughout the Confederate States.

Section 8, Clause 2: The Congress shall have power to borrow money on the credit of the Confederate States.

Section 8, Clause 3: The Congress shall have power to regulate commerce with foreign nations, and among the several States, and with the Indian tribes; but neither this, nor any other clause contained in the Constitution, shall ever be construed to delegate the power to Congress to appropriate money for any internal improvement intended to facilitate commerce; except for the purpose of furnishing lights, beacons, and buoys, and other aids to navigation upon the coasts, and the improvement of harbors and the removing of obstructions in river navigation; in all which cases such duties shall be laid on the navigation facilitated thereby as may be necessary to pay the costs and expenses thereof.

Section 8, Clause 4: The Congress shall have power to establish uniform laws of naturalization, and uniform laws on the subject of bankruptcies, throughout the Confederate States; but no law of Congress shall discharge any debt contracted before the passage of the same.

Section 8, Clause 5: The Congress shall have power to coin money, regulate the value thereof, and of foreign coin, and fix the standard of weights and measures.

Section 8, Clause 6: The Congress shall have power to provide for the punishment of counterfeiting the securities and current coin of the Confederate States.

CONFEDERATE GENERAL J.E.B. STUART.

Section 8, Clause 7: The Congress shall have power to establish post offices and post routes; but the expenses of the Post Office Department, after the 1st day of March in the year of our Lord eighteen hundred and sixty-three, shall be paid out of its own revenues.

Section 8, Clause 8: The Congress shall have power to promote the progress of science and useful arts, by securing for limited times to authors and inventors the exclusive right to their respective writings and discoveries.

Section 8, Clause 9: The Congress shall have power to constitute tribunals inferior to the Supreme Court.

Section 8, Clause 10: The Congress shall have power to define and punish piracies and felonies committed on the high seas, and offenses against the law of nations.

Section 8, Clause 11: The Congress shall have power to declare war, grant letters of marque and reprisal, and make rules concerning captures on land and water.

Section 8, Clause 12: The Congress shall have power to raise and support armies; but no appropriation of money to that use shall be for a longer term than two years.

Section 8, Clause 13: The Congress shall have power to provide and maintain a navy.

Section 8, Clause 14: The Congress shall have power to make rules for the government and regulation of the land and naval forces.

Section 8, Clause 15: The Congress shall have power to provide for calling forth the militia to execute the laws of the Confederate States, suppress insurrections, and repel invasions.

Section 8, Clause 16: The Congress shall have power to provide for organizing, arming, and disciplining the militia, and for governing such part of them as may be employed in the service of the Confederate States; reserving to the States, respectively, the appointment of the officers, and the authority of training the militia according to the discipline prescribed by Congress.

Section 8, Clause 17: The Congress shall have power to exercise exclusive legislation, in all cases whatsoever, over such district (not exceeding ten miles square) as may, by cession of one or more States and the acceptance of Congress, become the seat of the Government of the Confederate States; and to exercise like authority over all places purchased by the consent of the Legislature of the State in which the same shall be, for the erection of forts, magazines, arsenals, dockyards, and other needful buildings; and

Section 8, Clause 18: The Congress shall have power to make all laws which shall be necessary and proper for carrying into execution the foregoing powers, and all other powers vested by this Constitution in the Government of the Confederate States, or in any department or officer thereof.

Section 9, Clause 1: The importation of negroes of the African race from any foreign country other than the slaveholding States or Territories of the United States of America, is hereby forbidden; and Congress is required to pass such laws as shall effectually prevent the same.

Section 9, Clause 2: Congress shall also have power to prohibit the introduction of slaves from any State not a member of, or Territory not belonging to, this Confederacy.

Section 9, Clause 3: The privilege of the writ of habeas corpus shall not be suspended, unless when in cases of rebellion or invasion the public safety may require it.

Section 9, Clause 4: No bill of attainder, ex post facto law, or law denying or impairing the right of property in negro slaves shall be passed.

Section 9, Clause 5: No capitation or other direct tax shall be laid, unless in proportion to the census or enumeration hereinbefore directed to be taken.

Section 9, Clause 6: No tax or duty shall be laid on articles exported from any State, except by a vote of two-thirds of both Houses.

Section 9, Clause 7: No preference shall be given by any regulation of commerce or revenue to the ports of one State over those of another.

Section 9, Clause 8: No money shall be drawn from the Treasury, but in consequence of appropriations made by law; and a regular statement and account of the receipts and expenditures of all public money shall be published from time to time.

Section 9, Clause 9: Congress shall appropriate no money from the Treasury except by a vote of two-thirds of both Houses, taken by yeas and nays, unless it be asked and estimated for by some one of the heads of departments and submitted to Congress by the President; or for the purpose of paying its

BATTLE OF GLENDALE.

own expenses and contingencies; or for the payment of claims against the Confederate States, the justice of which shall have been judicially declared by a tribunal for the investigation of claims against the Government, which it is hereby made the duty of Congress to establish.

Section 9, Clause 10: All bills appropriating money shall specify in Federal currency the exact amount of each appropriation and the purposes for which it is made; and Congress shall grant no extra compensation to any public contractor, officer, agent, or servant, after such contract shall have been made or such service rendered.

Section 9, Clause 11: No title of nobility shall be granted by the Confederate States; and no person holding any office of profit or trust under them shall, without the consent of the Congress, accept of any present, emolument, office, or title of any kind whatever, from any king, prince, or foreign state.

Section 9, Clause 12: Congress shall make no law respecting an establishment of religion, or prohibiting the free exercise thereof; or abridging the freedom of speech, or of the press; or the right of the people peaceably to assemble and petition the Government for a redress of grievances.

Section 9, Clause 13: A well-regulated militia being necessary to the security of a free State, the right of the people to keep and bear arms shall not be infringed.

Section 9, Clause 14: No soldier shall, in time of peace, be quartered in any house without the consent of the owner; nor in time of war, but in a manner to be prescribed by law.

Section 9, Clause 15: The right of the people to be secure in their persons, houses, papers, and effects, against unreasonable searches and seizures, shall not be violated; and no warrants shall issue but upon probable cause, supported by oath or affirmation, and particularly describing the place to be searched and the persons or things to be seized.

Section 9, Clause 16: No person shall be held to answer for a capital or otherwise infamous crime, unless on a presentment or indictment of a grand jury, except in cases arising in the land or naval forces, or in the militia, when in actual service in time of war or public danger; nor shall any person be subject for the same offense to be twice put in jeopardy of life or limb; nor be compelled, in any criminal case, to be a witness against himself; nor be deprived of life, liberty, or property without due process of law; nor shall private property be taken for public use, without just compensation.

Section 9, Clause 17: In all criminal prosecutions the accused shall enjoy the right to a speedy and public trial, by an impartial jury of the State and district wherein the crime shall have been committed, which district shall have been previously ascertained by law, and to be informed of the nature and cause of the accusation; to be confronted with the witnesses against him; to have compulsory process for obtaining witnesses in his favor; and to have the assistance of counsel for his defense.

Section 9, Clause 18: In suits at common law, where the value in controversy shall exceed twenty dollars, the right of trial by jury shall be preserved; and no fact so tried by a jury shall be otherwise reexamined in any court of the Confederacy, than according to the rules of common law.

Section 9, Clause 19: Excessive bail shall not be required, nor excessive fines imposed, nor cruel and unusual punishments inflicted.

Section 9, Clause 20: Every law, or resolution having the force of law, shall relate to but one subject, and that shall be expressed in the title.

Section 10, Clause 1: No State shall enter into any treaty, alliance, or confederation; grant letters of marque and reprisal; coin money; make anything but gold and silver coin a tender in payment of debts; pass any bill of attainder, or ex post facto law, or law impairing the obligation of contracts; or grant any title of nobility.

BATTLE OF MALVERN HILL.

Section 10, Clause 2: No State shall, without the consent of the Congress, lay any imposts or duties on imports or exports, except what may be absolutely necessary for executing its inspection laws; and the net produce of all duties and imposts, laid by any State on imports, or exports, shall be for the use of the Treasury of the Confederate States; and all such laws shall be subject to the revision and control of Congress.

Section 10, Clause 3: No State shall, without the consent of Congress, lay any duty on tonnage, except on seagoing vessels, for the improvement of its rivers and harbors navigated by the said vessels; but such duties shall not conflict with any treaties of the Confederate States with foreign nations; and any surplus revenue thus derived shall, after making such improvement, be paid into the common treasury. Nor shall any State keep troops or ships of war in time of peace, enter into any agreement or compact with another State, or with a foreign power, or engage in war, unless actually invaded, or in such imminent danger as will not admit of delay. But when any river divides or flows through two or more States they may enter into compacts with each other to improve the navigation thereof.

ARTICLE 2

Section 1, Clause 1: The executive power shall be vested in a President of the Confederate States of America. He and the Vice President shall hold their offices for the term of six years; but the President shall not be reeligible. The President and Vice President shall be elected as follows:

Section 1, Clause 2: Each State shall appoint, in such manner as the Legislature thereof may direct, a number of electors equal to the whole number of Senators and Representatives to which the State may be entitled in the Congress; but no Senator or Representative or person holding an office of trust or profit under the Confederate States shall be appointed an elector.

Section 1, Clause 3: The electors shall meet in their respective States and vote by ballot for President and Vice President, one of whom, at least, shall not be an inhabitant of the same State with themselves; they shall name in their ballots the person voted for as President, and in distinct ballots the person voted for as Vice President, and they shall make distinct lists of all persons voted for as President, and of all persons voted for as Vice President, and of the number of votes for each, which lists they shall sign and certify, and transmit, sealed, to the seat of the Government of the Confederate States, directed to the President of the Senate; the President of the Senate shall, in the presence of the Senate and House of Representatives, open all the certificates, and the votes shall then be counted; the person having the greatest number of votes for President shall be the President, if such number be a majority of the whole number of electors appointed; and if no person have such majority, then from the persons having the highest numbers, not exceeding three, on the list of those voted for as President, the House of Representatives shall choose immediately, by ballot, the President. But in choosing the President the votes shall be taken by States, the representation from each State having one vote; a quorum for this purpose shall consist of a member or members from two-thirds of the States, and a majority of all the States shall be necessary to a choice. And if the House of Representatives shall not choose a President, whenever the right of choice shall devolve upon them, before the 4th day of March next following, then the Vice President shall act as President, as in case of the death, or other constitutional disability of the President.

Section 1, Clause 4: The person having the greatest number of votes as Vice President shall be the Vice President, if such number be a majority of the whole number of electors appointed; and if no person have a majority, then, from the two highest numbers on the list, the Senate shall choose the Vice President; a quorum for the purpose shall consist of two-thirds of the whole number of Senators, and a majority of the whole number shall be necessary to a choice.

Section 1, Clause 5: But no person constitutionally ineligible to the office of President shall be eligible to that of Vice President of the Confederate States.

Section 1, Clause 6: The Congress may determine the time of choosing the electors, and the day on which they shall give their votes; which day shall be the same throughout the Confederate States.

Section 1, Clause 7: No person except a natural-born citizen of the Confederate; States, or a citizen thereof at the time of the adoption of this Constitution, or a citizen thereof born in the United States prior to the 20th of December, 1860, shall be eligible to the office of President; neither shall any person be eligible to that office who shall not have attained the age of thirty-five years, and been fourteen years a resident within the limits of the Confederate States, as they may exist at the time of his election.

Section 1, Clause 8: In case of the removal of the President from office, or of his death, resignation, or inability to discharge the powers and duties of said office, the same shall devolve on the Vice President; and the Congress may, by law, provide for the case of removal, death, resignation, or inability, both of the President and Vice President, declaring what officer shall then act as President; and such officer shall act accordingly until the disability be removed or a President shall be elected.

CONFEDERATE STATESMAN JUDAH BENJAMIN.

Section 1, Clause 9: The President shall, at stated times, receive for his services a compensation, which shall neither be increased nor diminished during the period for which he shall have been elected; and he shall not receive within that period any other emolument from the Confederate States, or any of them.

Section 1, Clause 10: Before he enters on the execution of his office he shall take the following oath or affirmation: "I do solemnly swear (or affirm) that I will faithfully execute the office of President of the Confederate States, and will, to the best of my ability, preserve, protect, and defend the Constitution thereof."

Section 2, Clause 1: The President shall be Commander-in-Chief of the Army and Navy of the Confederate States, and of the militia of the several States, when called into the actual service of the Confederate

States; he may require the opinion, in writing, of the principal officer in each of the Executive Departments, upon any subject relating to the duties of their respective offices; and he shall have power to grant reprieves and pardons for offenses against the Confederate States, except in cases of impeachment.

Section 2, Clause 2: He shall have power, by and with the advice and consent of the Senate, to make treaties; provided two-thirds of the Senators present concur; and he shall nominate, and by and with the advice and consent of the Senate shall appoint, ambassadors, other public ministers and consuls, judges of the Supreme Court, and all other officers of the Confederate States whose appointments are not herein otherwise provided for, and which shall be established by law; but the Congress may, by law, vest the appointment of such inferior officers, as they think proper, in the President alone, in the courts of law, or in the heads of departments.

Section 2, Clause 3: The principal officer in each of the Executive Departments, and all persons connected with the diplomatic service, may be removed from office at the pleasure of the President. All other civil officers of the Executive Departments may be removed at any time by the President, or other appointing power, when their services are unnecessary, or for dishonesty, incapacity, inefficiency, misconduct, or neglect of duty; and when so removed, the removal shall be reported to the Senate, together with the reasons therefor.

Section 2, Clause 4: The President shall have power to fill all vacancies that may happen during the recess of the Senate, by granting commissions which shall expire at the end of their next session; but no person rejected by the Senate shall be reappointed to the same office during their ensuing recess.

Section 3, Clause 1: The President shall, from time to time, give to the Congress information of the state of the Confederacy, and recommend to their consideration such measures as he shall judge necessary and expedient; he may, on extraordinary occasions, convene both Houses, or either of them; and in case of disagreement between them, with respect to the time of adjournment, he may adjourn them to such time as he shall think proper; he shall receive ambassadors and other public ministers; he shall take care that the laws be faithfully executed, and shall commission all the officers of the Confederate States.

Section 4, Clause 1: The President, Vice President, and all civil officers of the Confederate States, shall be removed from office on impeachment for and conviction of treason, bribery, or other high crimes and misdemeanors.

ARTICLE 3

Section 1, Clause 1: The judicial power of the Confederate States shall be vested in one Supreme Court, and in such inferior courts as the Congress may, from time to time, ordain and establish. The judges, both of the Supreme and inferior courts, shall hold their offices during good behavior, and shall, at stated times, receive for their services a compensation which shall not be diminished during their continuance in office.

CONFEDERATE GENERAL ROBERT E. LEE.

Section 2, Clause 1: The judicial power shall extend to all cases arising under this Constitution, the laws of the Confederate States, and treaties made, or which shall be made, under their authority; to all cases affecting ambassadors, other public ministers and consuls; to all cases of admiralty and maritime jurisdiction; to controversies to which the Confederate States shall be a party; to controversies between two or more States; between a State and citizens of another State, where the State is plaintiff; between citizens claiming lands under grants of different States; and between a State or the citizens thereof, and foreign states, citizens, or subjects; but no State shall be sued by a citizen or subject of any foreign state.

Section 2, Clause 2: In all cases affecting ambassadors, other public ministers and consuls, and those in which a State shall be a party, the Supreme Court shall have original jurisdiction. In all the other cases before mentioned, the Supreme Court shall have appellate jurisdiction both as to law and fact, with such exceptions and under such regulations as the Congress shall make.

Section 2, Clause 3: The trial of all crimes, except in cases of impeachment, shall be by jury, and such trial shall be held in the State where the said crimes shall have been committed; but when not committed within any State, the trial shall be at such place or places as the Congress may by law have directed.

Section 3, Clause 1: Treason against the Confederate States shall consist only in levying war against them, or in adhering to their enemies, giving them aid and comfort. No person shall be convicted of treason unless on the testimony of two witnesses to the same overt act, or on confession in open court.

Section 3, Clause 2: The Congress shall have power to declare the punishment of treason; but no attainder of treason shall work corruption of blood, or forfeiture, except during the life of the person attainted.

ARTICLE 4

Section 1, Clause 1: Full faith and credit shall be given in each State to the public acts, records, and judicial proceedings of every other State; and the Congress may, by general laws, prescribe the manner in which such acts, records, and proceedings shall be proved, and the effect thereof.

Section 2, Clause 1: The citizens of each State shall be entitled to all the privileges and immunities of citizens in the several States; and shall have the right of transit and sojourn in any State of this Confederacy, with their slaves and other property; and the right of property in said slaves shall not be thereby impaired.

Section 2, Clause 2: A person charged in any State with treason, felony, or other crime against the laws of such State, who shall flee from justice, and be found in another State, shall, on demand of the executive authority of the State from which he fled, be delivered up, to be removed to the State having jurisdiction of the crime.

Section 2, Clause 3: No slave or other person held to service or labor in any State or Territory of the Confederate States, under the laws thereof, escaping or lawfully carried into another, shall, in consequence of any law or regulation therein, be discharged from such service or labor; but shall be delivered up on claim of the party to whom such slave belongs, or to whom such service or labor may be due.

Section 3, Clause 1: Other States may be admitted into this Confederacy by a vote of two-thirds of the whole House of Representatives and two-thirds of the Senate, the Senate voting by States; but no new State shall be formed or erected within the jurisdiction of any other State, nor any State be formed by the junction of two or more States, or parts of States, without the consent of the Legislatures of the States concerned, as well as of the Congress.

Section 3, Clause 2: The Congress shall have power to dispose of and make all needful rules and regulations concerning the property of the Confederate States, including the lands thereof.

Section 3, Clause 3: The Confederate States may acquire new territory; and Congress shall have power to legislate and provide governments for the inhabitants of all territory belonging to the Confederate States, lying without the limits of the several Sates; and may permit them, at such times, and in such manner as it may by law provide, to form States to be admitted into the Confederacy. In all such territory the institution of negro slavery, as it now exists in the Confederate States, shall be recognized and protected by Congress and by the Territorial government; and the inhabitants of the several Confederate States and Territories shall have the right to take to such Territory any slaves lawfully held by them in any of the States or Territories of the Confederate States.

CONFEDERATE GENERAL NATHAN BEDFORD FORREST.

Section 3, Clause 4: The Confederate States shall guarantee to every State that now is, or hereafter may become, a member of this Confederacy, a republican form of government; and shall protect each of them against invasion; and on application of the Legislature or of the Executive when the Legislature is not in session) against domestic violence.

ARTICLE 5
Section 1, Clause 1: Upon the demand of any three States, legally assembled in their several conventions, the Congress shall summon a convention of all the States, to take into consideration such amendments to the Constitution as the said States shall concur in suggesting at the time when the said demand is made; and should any of the proposed amendments to the Constitution be agreed on by the said convention, voting by States, and the same be ratified by the Legislatures of two- thirds of the several States, or by conventions in two-thirds thereof, as the one or the other mode of ratification may be proposed by the general convention, they shall thenceforward form a part of this Constitution. But no State shall, without its consent, be deprived of its equal representation in the Senate.

ARTICLE 6
Clause 1: The Government established by this Constitution is the successor of the Provisional Government of the Confederate States of America, and all the laws passed by the latter shall continue in force until the same shall be repealed or modified; and all the officers appointed by the same shall remain in office until their successors are appointed and qualified, or the offices abolished.

Clause 2: All debts contracted and engagements entered into before the adoption of this Constitution shall be as valid against the Confederate States under this Constitution, as under the Provisional Government.

Clause 3: This Constitution, and the laws of the Confederate States made in pursuance thereof, and all treaties made, or which shall be made, under the authority of the Confederate States, shall be the supreme law of the land; and the judges in every State shall be bound thereby, anything in the constitution or laws of any State to the contrary notwithstanding.

Clause 4: The Senators and Representatives before mentioned, and the members of the several State Legislatures, and all executive and judicial officers, both of the Confederate States and of the several States, shall be bound by oath or affirmation to support this Constitution; but no religious test shall ever be required as a qualification to any office or public trust under the Confederate States.

Clause 5: The enumeration, in the Constitution, of certain rights shall not be construed to deny or disparage others retained by the people of the several States.

Clause 6: The powers not delegated to the Confederate States by the Constitution, nor prohibited by it to the States, are reserved to the States, respectively, or to the people thereof.

ARTICLE 7

Clause 1: The ratification of the conventions of five States shall be sufficient for the establishment of this Constitution between the States so ratifying the same.

Clause 2: When five States shall have ratified this Constitution, in the manner before specified, the Congress under the Provisional Constitution shall prescribe the time for holding the election of President and Vice President; and for the meeting of the Electoral College; and for counting the votes, and inaugurating the President. They shall, also, prescribe the time for holding the first election of members of Congress under this Constitution, and the time for assembling the same. Until the assembling of such Congress, the Congress under the Provisional Constitution shall continue to exercise the legislative powers granted them; not extending beyond the time limited by the Constitution of the Provisional Government.

Adopted unanimously by the Congress of the Confederate States of South Carolina, Georgia, Florida, Alabama, Mississippi, Louisiana, and Texas, sitting in convention at the capitol, the city of Montgomery, Ala., on the eleventh day of March, in the year eighteen hundred and Sixty-one.[10]

Howell Cobb, President of the Congress.

SOUTH CAROLINA: R. Barnwell Rhett, C. G. Memminger, Wm. Porcher Miles, James Chesnut, Jr., R. W. Barnwell, William W. Boyce, Lawrence M. Keitt, T. J. Withers.

GEORGIA: Francis S. Bartow, Martin J. Crawford, Benjamin H. Hill, Thos. R. R. Cobb.

FLORIDA: Jackson Morton, J. Patton Anderson, Jas. B. Owens.

ALABAMA: Richard W. Walker, Robt. H. Smith, Colin J. McRae, William P. Chilton, Stephen F. Hale, David P. Lewis, Tho. Fearn, Jno. Gill Shorter, J. L. M. Curry.

MISSISSIPPI: Alex. M. Clayton, James T. Harrison, William S. Barry, W. S. Wilson, Walker Brooke, W. P. Harris, J. A. P. Campbell.

LOUISIANA: Alex. de Clouet, C. M. Conrad, Duncan F. Kenner, Henry Marshall.

TEXAS: John Hemphill, Thomas N. Waul, John H. Reagan, Williamson S. Oldham, Louis T. Wigfall, John Gregg, William Beck Ochiltree.

BATTLE OF WILSON'S CREEK.

BATTLE OF FORTS JACKSON AND ST. PHILIP.

Appendices
Supplemental Documents

SOME EARLY AMERICAN FLAGS.

APPENDIX A

Fairfax County Resolves

Adopted July 18, 1774
Alexandria, Virginia

- ☞ The Fairfax County Resolves were written two years before the Articles of Confederation, making them one of our earliest "rebellion" documents.
- ☞ Their authors were moderate Conservative George Washington and far-right Conservative George Mason, who penned the Resolves on July 17, 1774, at Mount Vernon.
- ☞ The Resolves emphasized the need for the colonies to form a constitutional association—that is, a confederacy—in an effort to put an end to the crushing dictatorial actions of Great Britain on the American colonies.
- ☞ Washington's and Mason's document aided in consolidating colonial sentiment against the royal crown, which in turn helped inspire the uprisings that led to both the American Revolutionary War and the formation of a new confederate republic: the United States of America, nicknamed "the Confederate States of America."

A T A GENERAL MEETING OF the Freeholders and Inhabitants of the County of Fairfax on Monday the 18th day of July 1774, at the Court House, George Washington Esquire Chairman, and Robert Harrison Gent: Clerk of the said Meeting.

1. Resolved that this Colony and Dominion of Virginia can not be considered as a conquered Country; and if it was, that the present Inhabitants are the Descendants not of the Conquered, but of the Conquerors.

That the same was not setled at the national Expence of England, but at the private Expence of the Adventurers, our Ancestors, by solemn Compact with, and under the Auspices and Protection of the British Crown; upon which We are in every Respect as dependant, as the People of Great Britain, and in the same Manner subject to all his Majesty's just, legal, and constitutional Prerogatives. That our Ancestors, when they left their native Land, and setled in America, brought with them (even if the same had not been confirmed by Charters) the Civil-Constitution and Form of Government of the Country they came from; and were by the Laws of Nature and Nations, entitled to all it's Privileges, Immunities and Advantages; which have descended to Us their Posterity, and ought of Right to be as fully enjoyed, as if We had still continued within the Realm of England.

2. Resolved that the most important and valuable Part of the British

Constitution, upon which it's very Existence depends, is the fundamental Principle of the People's being governed by no Laws, to which they have not given their Consent, by Representatives freely chosen by themselves; who are affected by the Laws they inact equally with their Constituents, to whom they are accountable, and whose Burthens they share; in which consists the Safety and Happiness of the Community: for if this Part of the Constitution was taken away, or materially altered, the Government must degenerate either into an absolute and despotic Monarchy, or a tyrannical Aristocracy, and the Freedom of the People be annihilated.

3. Resolved therefore, as the Inhabitants of the american Colonies are not, and from their Situation can not be represented in the British Parliament; that the legislative Power here can of Right be exercised only by our own provincial Assemblys or Parliaments, subject to the Assent or Negative of the British Crown, to be declared within some proper limited Time. But as it was thought just and reasonable that the People of Great Britain shou'd reap Advantages from these Colonies adequate to the Protection they afforded them, the British Parliament have claimed and exercised the Power of regulating our Trade and Commerce, so as to restrain our importing from foreign Countrys, such Articles as they cou'd furnish Us with, of their own Growth or Manufacture, or exporting to foreign Countrys such Articles and Portions of our Produce, as Great Britain stood in Need of, for her own Consumption or Manufactures. Such a Power directed with Wisdom and Moderation, seems necessary for the general Good of that great Body-politic of

GEORGE MASON.

which we are a Part; altho' in some Degree repugnant to the Principles of the Constitution. Under this Idea our Ancestors submitted to it; the Experience of more than a Century, during the Government of his Majesty's royal Predecessors, hath proved it's utility, and the reciprocal Benefits flowing from it produced mutual uninterrupted Harmony and Good-will, between the Inhabitants of Great Britain and her Colonies; who during that long Period, always considered themselves as one and the same People: and tho' such a Power is capable of Abuse, and in some Instances hath been stretched beyond the original Design and Institution, yet to avoid Strife and Contention with our fellow-Subjects, and strongly impressed with the Experience of mutual Benefits, We always Chearfully acquiesced in it, while the entire Regulation of our internal Policy, and giving and granting our own Money were preserved to our own provincial Legislatures.

4. Resolved that it is the Duty of these Colonies, on all Emergencies, to contribute, in proportion to their Abilities, Situation and Circumstances, to the necessary Charge of supporting and defending the British Empire, of which they are part; that while We are treated upon an equal Footing with our fellow subjects, the Motives of Self-Interest and Preservation will be a sufficient Obligation; as was evident thro' the Course of the last War; and that no Argument can be fairly applyed to the British Parliament's taxing us, upon a Presemption that We shou'd refuse a just and reasonable Contribution, but will equally operate in Justification of the Executive-Power taxing the People of England, upon a Supposition of their Representatives refusing to grant the necessary Supplies.

5. Resolved that the Claim lately assumed and exercised by the British Parliament of making all such Laws as they think fit, to govern the People of these Colonies, and to extort from Us our Money without our Consent, is not only diametrically contrary to the first Principles of the Constitution, and the original Compacts by which We are dependant upon the British Crown and Government; but is totally incompatible with the Privileges of a free People, and the natural Rights of Mankind; will render our own Legislatures merely nominal and nugatory, and is calculated to reduce Us from a State of Freedom and Happiness, to Slavery and Misery.

6. Resolved that Taxation and Representation are in their Nature inseperable; that the Right of withholding, or of giving and granting their own Money is the only effectual Security to a free people against the Incroachments of Despotism and Tyranny; and that whenever they yield the one, they must quickly fall a Prey to the other.

7. Resolved that the Powers over the People of America now claimed by the British House of Commons, in whose Election We have no Share, on whose Determinations We can have no Influence, whose Information must be always defective and often false, who in many Instances may have a seperate, and in some an opposite Interest to ours, and who are removed from those Impressions of Tenderness and Compassion arising from personal Intercourse and Connections, which soften the Rigours of the most despotic Governments, must if continued, establish the most grievous and intollerable Species of Tyranny and Oppression that ever was inflicted upon Mankind.

8. Resolved that it is our greatest Wish and Inclination, as well as Interest, to continue our Connection with, and Dependance upon the British Government; but tho' We are it's Subjects, we will use every Means which Heaven hath given Us to prevent our becoming it's Slaves.

9. Resolved that there is a premeditated Design and System, formed and

pursued by the British Ministry, to introduce an arbitrary Government into his Majesty's American Dominions; to which End they are artfully prejudicing our Sovereign, and inflaming the Minds of our fellow-Subjects in Great Britain, by propagating the most malevolent Falsehoods; particularly that there is an Intention in the American Colonies to set up for independant States; endeavouring at the same Time, by various Acts of Violence and Oppression, by sudden and repeated Dissolutions of our Assemblies, whenever they presume to examine the Illegality of ministerial Mandates, or deliberate on the violated Rights of their Constituents; and by breaking in upon the American Charters, to reduce Us to a State of Desperation, and dissolve the original Compacts by which our Ancestors bound themselves and their Posterity to remain dependant upon the British Crown: which Measures, unless effectually counteracted, will end in the Ruin both of Great Britain and her Colonies.

10. Resolved that the several Acts of Parliament for raising a Revenue upon the People of America without their Consent, the creating new and dangerous Jurisdictions here, the taking away our Trials by Jurys, the ordering Persons upon Criminal accusations, to be tried in another Country than that in which the Fact is charged to have been committed, the Act inflicting ministerial Vengeance upon the Town of Boston, and the two Bills lately brought into Parliament for abrogating the Charter of the Province of Massachusetts Bay, and for the protection and Encouragement of Murderers in the said Province, are Part of the above mentioned iniquitous System. That the Inhabitants of the Town of Boston are now suffering in the common Cause of all British America, and are justly entitled to it's Support and Assistance; and therefore that a Subscription ought imediatly to be opened, and proper Persons appointed, in every County of this Colony to purchase Provisions, and consign them to some Gentlemen of Character in Boston, to be distributed among the poorer Sort of People there.

BRITISH UNIFORM IN THE TIME OF THE AMERICAN REVOLUTION.

11. Resolved that We will cordially join with our Friends and Brethren of this and the other Colonies, in such Measures as shall be judged most

AMERICAN REVOLUTIONARY GENERAL PHILIP SCHUYLER.

effectual for procuring Redress of our Grievances, and that upon obtaining such Redress, if the Destruction of the Tea at Boston be regarded as an Invasion of private Property, We shall be willing to contribute towards paying the East India Company the Value: but as We consider the said Company as the Tools and Instrument of Oppression in the Hands of Government and the Cause of our present Distress, it is the Opinion of this Meeting that the People of these Colonies shou'd forbear all further Dealings with them, by refusing to purchase their Merchandize, until that Peace, Safety and Good-order, which they have disturbed, be perfectly restored. And that all Tea now in this Colony, or which shall be imported into it shiped before the first Day of September next shou'd be deposited in some Store house to be appointed by the respective Committees of each County, until a sufficient Sum of Money be raised by subscription to reimburse the Owners the Value, and then to be publickly burn'd and destroyed; and if the same is not paid for and destroyed as aforesaid, that it remain in the Custody of the said Committees, at the Risque of the owners, until the Act of Parliament imposing a Duty upon Tea for raising a Revenue in America be repealed; and imediatly afterwards be delivered unto the Several Proprietors thereof, their Agents or Attorneys.

12. Resolved that Nothing will so much contribute to defeat the pernicious Designs of the common Enemies of Great Britain and her Colonies as a firm Union of the latter; who ought to regard every Act of Violence or Oppression inflicted upon any one of them, as aimed at all; and to effect this desireable Purpose, that a Congress shou'd be appointed, to consist of Deputies from all the Colonies, to concert a general and uniform Plan for the Defence and Preservation of our common Rights, and continueing the Connection and Dependance of the said Colonies upon Great Britain, under a just, lenient, permanent, and constitutional Form of Government.

13. Resolved that our most sincere and cordial Thanks be given to the Patrons and Friends of Liberty in Great Britain, for their spirited and patriotick Conduct, in Support of our constitutional Rights and Privileges, and their generous Efforts to prevent the present Distress and Calamity of America.

14. Resolved that every little jarring Interest and Dispute, which has ever happened between these Colonies, shou'd be buried in eternal Oblivion; that all Manner of Luxury and Extravagance ought imediatly to be laid aside, as totally inconsistent with the threatning and gloomy Prospect before us; that it is the indispensable Duty of all the Gentlemen and Men of Fortune to set Examples of Temperance, Fortitude, Frugality and Industry; and give every Encouragement in their Power, particularly by Subscriptions and Premiums, to the Improvement of Arts and Manufactures in America; that great Care and Attention shou'd be had to the Cultivation of Flax, Cotton, and other Materials for Manufactures; and We recommend it to such of the Inhabitants who have large Stocks of Sheep, to sell to their Neighbours at a moderate Price, as the most certain Means of speedily increasing our Breed of Sheep, and Quantity of Wool.

WASHINGTON AND LAFAYETTE AT VALLEY FORGE WINTER OF 1777-1778.

15. Resolved that until american Grievances be redressed, by Restoration of our just Rights and Privileges, no Goods or Merchandize whatsoever ought to be imported into this Colony, which shall be shiped from Great Britain or Ireland after the first Day of September next, except Linnens not exceeding fifteen Pence [per] yard, coarse Woolen Cloth, not exceeding two shillings Sterling [per] yard, Nails, wire and Wire-Cards, needles & pins, paper, Salt petre and Medecines; which may be imported until the first Day of September one thousand seven hundred and seventy six; and if any Goods or Merchandize, other than those hereby excepted, shou'd be ship'd from Great Britain, after the

time aforesaid, to this Colony, that the same, imediately upon their Arrival shou'd either be sent back again, by the owners their Agents or Attorneys, or stored and deposited in some Warehouse, to be appointed by the Committee for each respective County, and there kept, at the Risque and Charge of the Owners, to be delivered to them, when a free Importation of Goods hither shall again take Place. And that the Merchants and Venders of Goods and Merchandize within this Colony ought not to take Advantage of our present Distress, but continue to sell the Goods and Merchandize which they now have, or which may be shiped to them before the first Day of September next, at the same rates and Prices they have been accustomed to do, within one Year last past; and if any Person shall sell such Goods on any other Terms than above expressed, that no Inhabitant of this Colony shou'd at any time, forever thereafter, deal with Him, his Agent, Factor, or Store keepers for any Commodity whatsoever.

16. Resolved that it is the Opinion of this Meeting that the Merchants and Venders of Goods and Merchandize within this Colony shou'd take an Oath not to sell or dispose of any Goods or Merchandize whatsoever, which may be shiped from Great Britain after the first Day of September next as aforesaid, except the Articles before excepted, and that they will, upon Receipt of such prohibited Goods, either send the same back again by the first Opportunity, or deliver them to the Committees in the respective Countys, to be deposited in some Warehouse, at the Risque and charge of the owners, until they, their Agents or Factors be permitted to take them away by the said Committees: the names of those who refuse to take such Oath to be advertized, by the respective Committees, in the Countys wherein they reside. And to the End that the Inhabitants of this Colony may know what Merchants, and Venders of Goods and Merchandize have taken such Oath, that the respective Committees shou'd grant a Certificate thereof to every such Person who shall take the same.

17. Resolved that it is the Opinion of this Meeting, that during our present Difficulties and Distress, no Slaves ought to be imported into any of the British Colonies on this Continent, and We take this Opportunity of declaring our most earnest Wishes to see an entire Stop for ever put to such a wicked cruel and unnatural Trade.

18. Resolved that no kind of Lumber shou'd be exported from this Colony to the West Indies until America be restored to her constitutional Rights and Liberties, if the other Colonies will accede to a like Resolution; and that it be recommended to the general Congress to appoint as early a Day as possible for stopping such Export.

19. Resolved that it is the Opinion of this Meeting, if american

Grievances be not redressed before the first Day of November one thousand seven hundred and seventy five, that all Exports of Produce from the several Colonies to Great Britain shou'd cease; and to carry the said Resolution more effectually into Execution, that We will not plant or cultivate any Tobacco after the Crop now growing, provided the same Measure shall be adopted by the other Colonies on this Continent, as well those who have heretofore made Tobacco, as those who have not. And it is our Opinion also, if the Congress of Deputies from the several Colonies shall adopt the Measure of Non-exportation to Great Britain, as the People will be thereby disabled from paying their Debts, that no Judgements shou'd be rendered by the Courts in the said Colonies for any Debt, after Information of the said Measures being determined upon.

AMERICAN REVOLUTIONARY GENERAL PETER MUHLENBURG.

20. Resolved that it is the Opinion of this Meeting that a solemn Covenant and Association shou'd be entered into by the Inhabitants of all the Colonies upon Oath, that they will not, after the Times which shall be respectively agreed on at the general Congress, export any Manner of Lumber to the West Indies, nor any of their Produce to Great Britain, or sell or dispose of the same to any Person who shall not have entered into the said Covenant and Association; and also that they will not import or receive any Goods or Merchandize which shall be ship'd from Great Britain after the first Day of September next, other than the before enumerated Articles, nor buy or purchase any Goods, except as before excepted, if any person whatsoever, who shall not have taken the Oath herein before recommended to be taken by the Merchants and Venders of Goods nor buy or purchase any Slaves hereafter imported into any part of this continent until a free Exportation and Importation be again resolved on by the Majority of the Representatives or Deputies of the Colonies. And that the respective Committees of the Countys in each Colony so soon as the Covenant and Association becomes general, publish by advertisements in their several Counties a List of the Names of those (if any such there be) who will not accede thereto; that such Traitors to their Country may be publickly known and detested.

21. Resolved that it is the Opinion of this Meeting, that this and the other associating Colonies shou'd break off all Trade, Intercourse, and Dealings, with that Colony Province or Town, which shall decline or refuse to agree to the plan which shall be adopted by the general Congress.

22. Resolved that shou'd the Town of Boston be forced to submit to the late cruel and oppressive Measures of Government, that We shall not hold the same to be binding upon Us, but will, notwithstanding, religiously maintain, and inviolably adhere to such Measures as shall be concerted by the general Congress, for the preservation of our Lives Liberties and Fortunes.

23. Resolved that it be recommended to the Deputies of the general Congress to draw up and transmit an humble and dutiful petition and Remonstrance to his Majesty, asserting with decent Firmness our just and constitutional Rights and Privileges lamenting the fatal Necessity of being compelled to enter into Measures disgusting to his Majesty and his Parliament, or injurious to our fellow Subjects in Great Britain; declaring, in the strongest Terms, our Duty and Affection to his Majesty's Person, Family and Government, and our Desire to continue our Dependance upon Great Britain; and most humbly conjuring and beseeching his Majesty, not to reduce his faithful Subjects of America to a State of Desperation, and to reflect, that from our Sovereign there can be but one Appeal.

And it is the Opinion of this Meeting, that after such Petition, and Remonstrance shall have been presented to his Majesty, the same shou'd be printed in the public Papers, in all the principal Towns in Great Britain.

24. Resolved that George Washington Esquire and Charles Broadwater Gent. lately elected our Representatives to serve in the general Assembly, be appointed to attend the Convention at Williamsburgh, on the first Day of August next, and present these Resolves, as the Sense of the People of this County, upon the Measures proper to be taken in the present alarming and dangerous Situation of America.

BATTLE OF CAMDEN.

CAMP-FIRE AT SARATOGA.

APPENDIX B
The Lee Resolution
Introduced June 7, 1776

☞ Author of the Lee Resolution: Richard Henry Lee, Conservative U.S. Founding Father, 6th President of the United States under Confederation, and 1st cousin of Conservative Confederate General Robert E. Lee.

☞ On June 7, 1776, at the 2nd Continental Congress, R. H. Lee made a motion for the American colonies to declare independence from Great Britain and form a confederacy. The Resolution's final approval on July 2, 1776, helped launch the creation of the Articles of Confederation, the first constitution of the U.S.A.—not a "nation" or a "democracy," but a republic, one that George Washington referred to very specifically as a "*confederate* republic." The significance of the Lee Resolution was overshadowed two days later, July 4, 1776, when Thomas Jefferson's Declaration of Independence was adopted.

RESOLVED, THAT THESE UNITED COLONIES are, and of right ought to be, free and independent States, that they are absolved from all allegiance to the British Crown, and that all political connection between them and the State of Great Britain is, and ought to be, totally dissolved.

That it is expedient forthwith to take the most effectual measures for forming foreign Alliances.

That a plan of confederation be prepared and transmitted to the respective Colonies for their consideration and approbation.

RICHARD HENRY LEE.

THE EVENING BEFORE THE BATTLE OF BUNKER HILL.

APPENDIX C

Virginia Declaration of Rights

June 12, 1776

- ☞ Drafted by Conservative U.S. Founding Father George Mason.
- ☞ The Virginia Declaration of Rights (or Bill of Rights) was adopted unanimously June 12, 1776, by the 5th Virginia convention at Williamsburg.
- ☞ The Virginia Declaration of Rights was later appended to Virginia's state constitution, which itself was adopted on June 29, 1776.
- ☞ Mason was a major critic of the U.S. Constitution, which he (correctly) felt gave too much control and power to the national government. His concerns led to the development of the all-important Bill of Rights (the seeds which can be seen here), which added further restrictions to the national government while further empowering the individual states. The Bill of Rights (drafted and written by James Madison) was appended to the U.S. Constitution as the first Ten Amendments on Dec. 15, 1791.

A DECLARATION OF RIGHTS MADE BY the Representatives of the good people of Virginia, assembled in full and free Convention; which rights do pertain to them and their posterity, as the basis and foundation of Government.

ARTICLE 1: That all men are by nature equally free and independent, and have certain inherent rights, of which, when they enter into a state of society, they cannot, by any compact, deprive or divest their posterity; namely, the enjoyment of life and liberty, with the means of acquiring and possessing property, and pursuing and obtaining happiness and safety.

ARTICLE 2: That all power is vested in, and consequently derived from, the people; that magistrates are their trustees and servants, and at all times amenable to them.

ARTICLE 3: That government is, or ought to be, instituted for the common benefit, protection, and security of the people, nation or community; of all the various modes and forms of government that is best, which is capable of producing the greatest degree of happiness and safety and is most effectually secured against the danger of maladministration; and that, whenever any government shall be found inadequate or contrary to these purposes, a majority of the community hath an indubitable, unalienable, and indefeasible right to reform, alter or abolish it, in such manner as shall be judged most conducive to the public weal.

ARTICLE 4: That no man, or set of men, are entitled to exclusive or separate emoluments or privileges from the community, but in consideration of public services; which, not being descendible, neither ought the offices of magistrate, legislator, or judge be hereditary.

ARTICLE 5: That the legislative and executive powers of the state should be separate and distinct from the judicative; and, that the members of the two first may be restrained from oppression by feeling and participating the burthens of the people, they should, at fixed periods, be reduced to a private station, return into that body from which they were originally taken, and the vacancies be supplied by frequent, certain, and regular elections in which all, or any part of the former members, to be again eligible, or ineligible, as the laws shall direct.

ARTICLE 6: That elections of members to serve as representatives of the people in assembly ought to be free; and that all men, having sufficient evidence of permanent common interest with, and attachment to, the community have the right of suffrage and cannot be taxed or deprived of their property for public uses without their own consent or that of their representatives so elected, nor bound by any law to which they have not, in like manner, assented, for the public good.

ARTICLE 7: That all power of suspending laws, or the execution of laws, by any authority without consent of the representatives of the people is injurious to their rights and ought not to be exercised.

ARTICLE 8: That in all capital or criminal prosecutions a man hath a right to demand the cause and nature of his accusation to be confronted with the accusers and witnesses, to call for evidence in his favor, and to a speedy trial by an impartial jury of his vicinage, without whose unanimous consent he cannot be found guilty, nor can he be compelled to give evidence against himself; that no man be deprived of his liberty except by the law of the land or the judgement of his peers.

ARTICLE 9: That excessive bail ought not to be required, nor excessive fines imposed; nor cruel and unusual punishments inflicted.

ARTICLE 10: That general warrants, whereby any officer or messenger may be commanded to search suspected places without evidence of a fact committed, or to seize any person or persons not named, or whose offense is not particularly described and supported by evidence, are grievous and oppressive and ought not to be granted.

ARTICLE 11: That in controversies respecting property and in suits between man and man, the ancient trial by jury is preferable to any other and ought to be held sacred.

ARTICLE 12: That the freedom of the press is one of the greatest bulwarks of liberty and can never be restrained but by despotic governments.

ARTICLE 13: That a well regulated militia, composed of the body of the people, trained to arms, is the proper, natural, and safe defense of a free state; that standing armies, in time of peace, should be avoided as dangerous to liberty; and that, in all cases, the military should be under strict subordination to, and be governed by, the civil power.

ARTICLE 14: That the people have a right to uniform government; and therefore, that no government separate from, or independent of, the government of Virginia, ought to be erected or established within the limits thereof.

ARTICLE 15: That no free government, or the blessings of liberty, can be preserved to any people but by a firm adherence to justice, moderation, temperance, frugality, and virtue and by frequent recurrence to fundamental principles.

ARTICLE 16: That religion, or the duty which we owe to our Creator and the manner of discharging it, can be directed by reason and conviction, not by force or violence; and therefore, all men are equally entitled to the free exercise of religion, according to the dictates of conscience; and that it is the mutual duty of all to practice Christian forbearance, love, and charity towards each other.

THE CAPTURE OF BRITISH MAJOR JOHN ANDRÉ.

THE OLD COURTHOUSE AT YORK, PENNSYLVANIA.

APPENDIX D

Rough Draft of the Declaration of Independence

Written June 1776

☛ Written by a "Committee of Five" appointed by the Continental Congress. Its members were: Thomas Jefferson of Virginia (the chief author), Benjamin Franklin of Pennsylvania, John Adams of Massachusetts, Robert Livingston of New York, and Roger Sherman of Connecticut.

☛ This revolutionary document was written primarily to explain to the world the multiple reasons the American colonies possessed the right to rebel against and secede from Great Britain (which included a list of serious grievances against King George III). Simultaneously, it was also designed to unify the colonies, whip up domestic and foreign support, and announce the formation of a new and independent "confederate republic," informally known as the Confederate States of America, and officially called the United States of America.

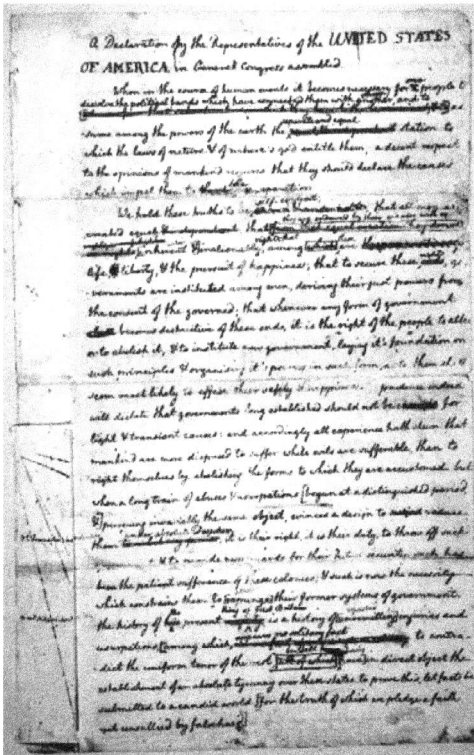

ORIGINAL ROUGH DRAFT OF THE DEC. OF INDEPENDENCE.

A DECLARATION BY THE REPRESENTATIVES OF United States of America, in General Congress Assembled.

When, in the course of human events, it becomes necessary for a people to advance from that subordination in which they have hitherto remained, and to assume among the powers of the earth, the equal and independent station to which the laws of nature and of nature's god entitle them, a decent respect to the opinions of mankind requires that they should declare the causes which impel them to the change

AMERICAN REVOLUTIONARY COMMANDER GENERAL DANIEL MORGAN.

We hold these truths to be self-evident, that all men are created equal and independent; that from that equal creation they derive in rights inherent and inalienables, among which are the preservation of life, and liberty and the pursuit of happiness; that to secure these ends, governments are instituted among men, deriving their just powers from the consent of the governed; that whenever any form of government shall become destructive of these ends, it is the right of the people to alter or to abolish it, and to institute new government, laying its foundation on such principles and organizing its powers in such form, as to them shall seem most likely to effect their safety and happiness. Prudence, indeed, will dictate that governments long established should not be changed for light and transient causes: and accordingly all experience hath shewn that mankind are more disposed to suffer while evils are sufferable, than to right themselves by abolishing the forms to which they are accustomed. But when a long train of abuses and usurpations, begun at a distinguished period, and pursuing invariably the same object evinces a design to reduce them to arbitrary power, it is their right, it is their duty, to throw off such government, and to provide new guards for their future security.

Such has been the patient sufferance of these colonies; and such is now the necessity which constrains them to expunge their former systems of government. The history of his present majesty [King George III] is a history of unremitting injuries and usurpations, among which no fact stands single or solitary to contradict the uniform tenor of the rest, all of which have in direct object the establishment of an absolute tyranny over these states. To prove this, let facts be submitted to a candid world, for the truth of which we pledge a faith yet unsullied by falsehood.

He has refused his assent to laws, the most wholesome and necessary for the public good.

He has forbidden his governors to pass laws of immediate and pressing importance, unless suspended in their operation till his assent should be obtained; and when so suspended, he has neglected utterly to attend to them.

He has refused to pass other laws for the accommodation of large districts of people unless those people would relinquish the right of representation in the legislature, a right inestimable to them and formidable to tyrants only.

He has dissolved representative houses repeatedly, for opposing with manly firmness his invasions on the rights of the people.

He has refused for a long space of time, to cause others to be elected, whereby the legislative powers, incapable of annihilation, have returned to the people at large for their exercise, the state remaining in the meantime exposed to all the dangers of invasion from without, and convulsions within.

He has endeavored to prevent the population of these states; for that purpose obstructing the laws for naturalization of foreigners; refusing to pass others to encourage their migration hither, and raising the conditions of new appropriations of lands.

He has suffered the administration of justice totally to cease in some of these colonies, refusing his assent to laws for establishing judiciary powers.

He has made our judges dependent on his will alone, for the tenure of their offices, and the amount of their salaries.

He has erected a multitude of new offices by a self-assumed power, and sent hither swarms of officers to harrass our people, and eat out their substance.

He has kept among us, in times of peace, standing armies and ships of war.

He has affected to render the military, independent of and superior to civil power.

He has combined with others to subject us to a jurisdiction foreign to our constitutions, and unacknowledged by our laws; giving his assent to their pretended acts of legislation:

> for quartering large bodies of armed troops among us;

> for protecting them, by mock trial, from punishment for any murders which they should commit on the inhabitants of these states;

> for cutting off our trade with all parts of the world;

> for imposing taxes on us without our consent;

> for depriving us of the benefits of trial by jury;

> for transporting us beyond seas to be tried for pretended offenses;

> for taking away our charters, and altering fundamentally the forms of our governments;

> for suspending our own legislatures, and declaring themselves invested with power to legislate for us in all cases whatsoever.

He has abdicated government here, withdrawing his governors, and declaring us out of his alegiance and protection.

He has plundered our seas, ravaged our coasts, burnt our towns, and destroyed the lives of our people.

He is at this time transporting large armies of foreign mercenaries to compleat the works of death, desolation and tyranny, already begun with circumstances of cruelty and perfidy unworthy the head of a civilized nation.

NATIVE AMERICANS ENLISTED BY THE BRITISH ATTACKING EUROPEAN AMERICANS DURING THE REVOLUTIONARY WAR, AN ATROCITY MENTIONED BY THOMAS JEFFERSON IN THE DECLARATION OF INDEPENDENCE.

He has endeavored to bring on the inhabitants of our frontiers the merciless Indian savages, whose known rule of warfare is an undistinguished destruction of all ages, sexes and conditions of existence:

He has incited treasonable insurrections of our fellow citizens with the allurements of forfeiture and confiscation of our property.

He has waged cruel war against human nature itself, violating it's most sacred rights of life and liberty in the persons of a distant people who never offended him, captivating and carrying them into slavery in another hemispere, or to incure miserable death in their transportation hither. This piratical warfare, the opprobium of infidel powers, is the warfare of the Christian king of Great Britain. Determined to keep open a market where MEN should be bought and sold, he has prostituted his negative for suppressing every legislative attempt to prohibit or to restrain this execrable commerce: and that this assemblage of horrors might want no fact of distinguished die, he is now exciting those very people to rise in arms among us, and to purchase that liberty of which he had deprived them, by murdering the people upon whom he also obtruded them; thus paying off former crimes committed against the liberties of one people, with crimes which he urges them to commit against the lives of another.

In every stage of these oppressions we have petitioned for redress in the most humble terms: our repeated petitions have been answered only by repeated injury.

A prince, whose character is thus marked by every act which may define a tyrant, is unfit to be the ruler of a people who mean to be free. Future ages will scarce believe that the hardiness of one man, adventured within the short compass of twelve years only, on so many acts of tyranny without a mask, over a people fostered and fixed in principles of liberty.

Nor have we been wanting in attention to our British brethren. We have warned them from time to time of attempts by their legislature to extend an unwarrantable jurisdiction over these our states. We have reminded them of the circumstances of our emigration and settlement here, no one of which could warrant so strange a pretension: that these were effected at the expence of our own blood and treasure, unassisted by the wealth or the strength of Great Britain: that in constituting indeed our several forms of government, we had adopted one common king, thereby laying a foundation for perpetual league and amity with them: but that submission to their parliament was no part of our constitution, nor ever in idea, if history may be credited: and we appealed to their native justice and magnanimity, as well as to the ties of our common kindred to disavow these usurpations, which were likely to interrupt our correspondence and connections. They too have been deaf to the voice of justice and of consanguinity, and when occasions have been given them, by the regular course of their laws, of removing from their councils the disturbers of our harmony, they have by their free election re-established them in power. At this very time too they are permitting their chief magistrate to send over not only soldiers of our common blood, but Scotch and foreign mercenaries to invade and deluge us in blood. These facts have given the last stab to agonizing affection, and manly spirit bids us to renounce forever these unfeeling brethren. We must endeavor to forget our former love for them, and hold them, as we hold the rest of mankind, enemies in war, in peace friends. We might have been a free and a great people together; but a communication of grandeur and of freedom it seems is below their dignity. Be it so, since they will have it: the road to happiness and to glory is open to us too. We will tread it apart from them and acquiesce in the necessity which denounces our eternal separation!

We, therefore, the representatives of the United States of America, in General Congress, assembled do, in the name, and by the authority of the good people of these states, reject and renounce the allegiance and subjection to the kings of Great Britain and all others who may hereafter claim by, through, or under them; we utterly dissolve and break off all political connection which may have heretofore subsisted between us and the people or parliament of Great Britain; and finally we do assert and declare these colonies to be free and independent states, and that as free and independent states they shall hereafter have full power to levy war, conclude peace, contract alliances, establish commerce, and to do all other acts and things which independent states may of right do.

And for the support of this declaration we mutually pledge to each other our lives, our fortunes and our sacred honor.

THE SURRENDER OF BRITISH GENERAL JOHN BURGOYNE AT SARATOGA.

APPENDIX E

Declaration of Independence

In Congress, July 4, 1776

☛ This, the final version, expounded on the theory of natural rights, justified the American colonists' role in the Revolutionary War, and gave birth to the confederate republic officially called the United States of America, and unofficially known as the Confederate States of America.

☛ While most of Thomas Jefferson's "long train of abuses and usurpations" against King George III were carried over from the rough draft, his blistering denunciation of slavery, as well as his scathing comments about Britain's imposition of slavery on the American colonies (an institution that, like nearly all Southerners, he viewed as an "execrable commerce"), were removed from this the final version.

☛ According to Jefferson himself, he was pressured by his cohorts to discard the slavery clause because, being the birthplace of American slavery, the Northeast was home to thousands of Yankees who were still actively financially involved in the "peculiar institution." Thus it was thought best not to poke the hornet's nest.

☛ The final version of the Declaration of Independence was signed by 56 delegates from 13 colonies (which later became states).

ORIGINAL DECLARATION OF INDEPENDENCE.

THE UNANIMOUS DECLARATION OF THE thirteen united States of America,

When in the Course of human events, it becomes necessary for one people to dissolve the political bands which have connected them with another, and to assume among the powers of the earth, the separate and equal station to which the Laws of Nature and of Nature's God entitle them, a decent respect to the opinions of mankind requires that they should declare the causes which impel them to the separation.

We hold these truths to be self-evident, that all men are created equal, that they are endowed by their Creator with certain unalienable Rights, that among these are Life, Liberty and the pursuit of Happiness.—That to secure these rights, Governments are instituted among Men, deriving their just powers from the consent of the governed,—That whenever any Form of Government becomes destructive of these ends, it is the Right of the People to alter or to abolish it, and to institute new Government, laying its foundation on such principles and organizing its powers in such form, as to them shall seem most likely to effect their Safety and Happiness. Prudence, indeed, will dictate that Governments long established should not be changed for light and transient causes; and accordingly all experience hath shewn, that mankind are more disposed to suffer, while evils are sufferable, than to right themselves by abolishing the forms to which they are accustomed. But when a long train of abuses and usurpations, pursuing invariably the same Object evinces a design to reduce them under absolute Despotism, it is their right, it is their duty, to throw off such Government, and to provide new Guards for their future security.—Such has been the patient sufferance of these Colonies; and such is now the necessity which constrains them to alter their former Systems of Government. The history of the present King of Great Britain [George III] is a history of repeated injuries and usurpations, all having in direct object the establishment of an absolute Tyranny over these States. To prove this, let Facts be submitted to a candid world.

He has refused his Assent to Laws, the most wholesome and necessary for the public good.

He has forbidden his Governors to pass Laws of immediate and pressing importance, unless suspended in their operation till his Assent should be obtained; and when so suspended, he has utterly neglected to attend to them.

He has refused to pass other Laws for the accommodation of large districts of people, unless those people would relinquish the right of Representation in the Legislature, a right inestimable to them and formidable to tyrants only.

He has called together legislative bodies at places unusual, uncomfortable, and distant from the depository of their public Records, for the sole purpose of fatiguing them into compliance with his measures.

He has dissolved Representative Houses repeatedly, for opposing with manly firmness his invasions on the rights of the people.

AMERICAN REVOLUTIONARY OFFICER COLONEL SAMUEL MILES.

He has refused for a long time, after such dissolutions, to cause others to be elected; whereby the Legislative powers, incapable of Annihilation, have returned to the People at large for their exercise; the State remaining in the mean time exposed to all the dangers of invasion from without, and convulsions within.

He has endeavoured to prevent the population of these States; for that purpose obstructing the Laws for Naturalization of Foreigners; refusing to pass others to encourage their migrations hither, and raising the conditions of new Appropriations of Lands.

He has obstructed the Administration of Justice, by refusing his Assent to Laws for establishing Judiciary powers.

He has made Judges dependent on his Will alone, for the tenure of their offices, and the amount and payment of their salaries.

He has erected a multitude of New Offices, and sent hither swarms of Officers to harrass our people, and eat out their substance.

He has kept among us, in times of peace, Standing Armies without the Consent of our legislatures.

He has affected to render the Military independent of and superior to the Civil power.

He has combined with others to subject us to a jurisdiction foreign to our constitution, and unacknowledged by our laws; giving his Assent to their Acts of pretended Legislation:

For Quartering large bodies of armed troops among us:

For protecting them, by a mock Trial, from punishment for any Murders which they should commit on the Inhabitants of these States:

For cutting off our Trade with all parts of the world:

For imposing Taxes on us without our Consent:

For depriving us in many cases, of the benefits of Trial by Jury:

For transporting us beyond Seas to be tried for pretended offences:

For abolishing the free System of English Laws in a neighbouring Province, establishing therein an Arbitrary government, and enlarging its Boundaries so as to render it at once an example and fit instrument for introducing the same absolute rule into these Colonies:

For taking away our Charters, abolishing our most valuable Laws, and altering fundamentally the Forms of our Governments:

For suspending our own Legislatures, and declaring themselves invested with power to legislate for us in all cases whatsoever.

He has abdicated Government here, by declaring us out of his Protection and waging War against us.

He has plundered our seas, ravaged our Coasts, burnt our towns, and destroyed the lives of our people.

He is at this time transporting large Armies of foreign Mercenaries to compleat the works of death, desolation and tyranny, already begun with circumstances of Cruelty & perfidy scarcely paralleled in the most barbarous ages, and totally unworthy the Head of a civilized nation.

He has constrained our fellow Citizens taken Captive on the high Seas to bear Arms against their Country, to become the executioners of their friends and Brethren, or to fall themselves by their Hands.

He has excited domestic insurrections amongst us, and has endeavoured to bring on the inhabitants of our frontiers, the merciless Indian Savages, whose known rule of warfare, is an undistinguished destruction of all ages, sexes and conditions.

In every stage of these Oppressions We have Petitioned for Redress in the most humble terms: Our repeated Petitions have been answered only by repeated injury. A Prince whose character is thus marked by every act which may define a Tyrant, is unfit to be the ruler of a free people.

Nor have We been wanting in attentions to our Brittish brethren. We have warned them from time to time of attempts by their legislature to extend an unwarrantable jurisdiction over us. We have reminded them of the circumstances of our emigration and settlement here. We have appealed to their native justice and magnanimity, and we have conjured them by the ties of our common kindred to disavow these usurpations, which, would inevitably interrupt our connections and correspondence. They too have been deaf to the voice of justice and of consanguinity. We must, therefore, acquiesce in the necessity, which denounces our Separation, and hold them, as we hold the rest of mankind, Enemies in War, in Peace Friends.

JOHN HANCOCK.

We, therefore, the Representatives of the united States of America, in General Congress, Assembled, appealing to the Supreme Judge of the world for the rectitude of our intentions, do, in the Name, and by Authority of the good People of these Colonies, solemnly publish and declare, That these United Colonies are, and of Right ought to be Free and Independent States; that they are Absolved from all Allegiance to the British Crown, and that all political connection between them and the State of Great Britain, is and ought to be totally dissolved; and that as Free and Independent States, they have full Power to levy War, conclude Peace, contract Alliances, establish Commerce, and to do all other Acts and Things which Independent States may of right do. And for the support of this Declaration, with a firm reliance on the protection of divine Providence, we mutually pledge to each other our Lives, our Fortunes and our sacred Honor.

GEORGIA: Button Gwinnett, Lyman Hall, George Walton.

NORTH CAROLINA: William Hooper, Joseph Hewes, John Penn.

SOUTH CAROLINA: Edward Rutledge, Thomas Heyward, Jr., Thomas Lynch, Jr., Arthur Middleton.

MARYLAND: Samuel Chase, William Paca, Thomas Stone, Charles Carroll of Carrollton.

VIRGINIA: George Wythe, Richard Henry Lee, Thomas Jefferson, Benjamin Harrison, Thomas Nelson, Jr., Francis Lightfoot Lee, Carter Braxton.

PENNSYLVANIA: Robert Morris, Benjamin Rush, Benjamin Franklin, John Morton, George Clymer, James Smith, George Taylor, James Wilson, George Ross.

DELAWARE: Caesar Rodney, George Read, Thomas McKean.

NEW YORK: William Floyd, Philip Livingston, Francis Lewis, Lewis Morris.

NEW JERSEY: Richard Stockton, John Witherspoon, Francis Hopkinson, John Hart, Abraham Clark.

NEW HAMPSHIRE: Josiah Bartlett, William Whipple, Matthew Thornton.

MASSACHUSETTS: John Hancock, Samuel Adams, John Adams, Robert Treat Paine, Elbridge Gerry.

RHODE ISLAND: Stephen Hopkins, William Ellery.

CONNECTICUT: Roger Sherman, Samuel Huntington, William Williams, Oliver Wolcott.

RETREAT FROM LONG ISLAND.

APPENDIX F
Washington's General Orders
Issued July 9, 1776

☛ Issued by George Washington to His Troops in the Summer of 1776.

HEAD QUARTERS, NEW YORK, JULY 9TH 1776.
PAROLE MANCHESTER. COUNTERSIGN NORFOLK.

John Evans of Capt: Ledyards Company Col. McDougall's Regiment—Hopkins Rice of Capt: Pierce's Company Col. Ritzema's Regiment having been tried by a General Court Martial whereof Col. Read was President and found guilty of "Desertion," were sentenced to receive each Thirty-nine Lashes. The General approves the Sentences and orders them to be executed at the usual time & place.

BATTLE OF BENNINGTON.

Passes to go from the City are hereafter to be granted by John Berrien, Henry Wilmot and John Ray Junr a Committee of the City appointed for that purpose—Officers of the Guards at the Ferries and Wharves, to be careful in making this regulation known to the sentries, who are to see that the passes are signed by one of the above persons, and to be careful no Soldier goes over the Ferry without a pass from a General officer.

The North River Guard to be removed to the Market House near the Ferry-Stairs, as soon as it is fitted up.

The Honorable Continental Congress having been pleased to allow a Chaplain to each Regiment, with the pay of Thirty-three Dollars and one third per month—The Colonels or commanding officers of each regiment are directed to procure Chaplains accordingly; persons of good Characters and exemplary lives—To see that all inferior officers and soldiers pay them a suitable respect and attend carefully upon religious exercises: The blessing and protection of Heaven are at all times necessary but especially so in times of public distress and danger—The

General hopes and trusts, that every officer, and man, will endeavour so to live, and act, as becomes a Christian Soldier defending the dearest Rights and Liberties of his country.

The Honorable the Continental Congress, impelled by the dictates of duty, policy and necessity, having been pleased to dissolve the Connection which subsisted between this Country, and Great Britain, and to declare the United Colonies of North America, free and independent STATES: The several brigades are to be drawn up this evening on their respective Parades, at six o clock, when the declaration of Congress, shewing the grounds & reasons of this measure, is to be read with an audible voice.

The General hopes this important Event will serve as a fresh incentive to every officer, and soldier, to act with Fidelity and Courage, as knowing that now the peace and safety of his Country depends (under God) solely on the success of our arms: And that he is now in the service of a State, possessed of sufficient power to reward his merit, and advance him to the highest Honors of a free Country.

The Brigade Majors are to receive, at the Adjutant Generals Office, several of the Declarations to be delivered to the Brigadiers General, and the Colonels of regiments.

The Brigade Majors are to be excused from farther attendance at Head Quarters, except to receive the Orders of the day, that their time and attention may be withdrawn as little as possible, from the duties of their respective brigades.

WASHINGTON CROSSING THE DELAWARE RIVER.

APPENDIX G

Kentucky & Virginia Resolutions

1798 & 1799

The Kentucky Resolution of 1798

December 24, 1798

- ☛ First drafted in October 1798 by small government Conservative Thomas Jefferson, who would be elected the third president of the U.S. two years later (in 1800). Authorship was kept secret at the time for fear that Jefferson might be arrested on charges of sedition.
- ☛ Written as a Conservative response to what was perceived as the "unconstitutional" and "obnoxious" Alien and Sedition Acts of 1798.
- ☛ Jefferson vigorously argued against the Left-wing inspired Acts, which made it a crime ("sedition") to denigrate the national government, Congress, or the president. This, of course, violates both state constitutions and the 1st Amendment of the U.S. Constitution guaranteeing freedom of speech. Jefferson emphasized the fact that the U.S. is built on a constitutional "compact" (a loose arrangement between sovereign nation-states), one overseen by a national government with delegated powers that do not permit it to "transgress the limits fixed by that compact."
- ☛ Jefferson's Resolution, which calls the Alien and Sedition Acts "unauthoritative, void, and of no force," was passed by the Kentucky House of Representatives on November 10, 1798, and agreed to by the Kentucky Senate on December 24, 1798. Unfortunately for the U.S., a majority of the other states rejected the Resolution as a "threat to the Union." And while the Acts eventually expired (after Jefferson's election in 1800), power continued to consolidate in Washington and weaken at the state level, the socialist outcome of which, today, is obvious to all.
- ☛ Note that both the Kentucky and the Virginia Resolutions later not only influenced passionate Southern proponent John C. Calhoun and his views on the doctrine of nullification, but they also had a profound impact on pro-States' rights sentiment during the secession of the Southern states in 1860 and 1861.

NOVEMBER 10, 1798 (PRINTED)

1. RESOLVED, THAT THE SEVERAL STATES composing the United States of America are not united on the principle of unlimited submission to their general government; but that, by compact, under the style and title of a Constitution for the United States, and of amendments thereto, they constituted a general government for special purposes, delegated to that government certain definite powers, reserving, each state to itself,

the residuary mass of right to their own self-government; and that whensoever the general government assumes undelegated powers, its acts are unauthoritative, void, and of no force; that to this compact each state acceded as a state, and is an integral party; that this government, created by this compact, was not made the exclusive or final judge of the extent of the powers delegated to itself, since that would have made its discretion, and not the Constitution, the measure of its powers; but that, as in all other cases of compact among parties having no common judge, each party has an equal right to judge for itself, as well of infractions as of the mode and measure of redress.

THOMAS JEFFERSON.

2. Resolved, That the Constitution of the United States having delegated to Congress a power to punish treason, counterfeiting the securities and current coin of the United States, piracies and felonies committed on the high seas, and offences against the laws of nations, and no other crimes whatever; and it being true, as a general principle, and one of the amendments to the Constitution having also declared "that the powers not delegated to the United States by the Constitution, nor prohibited by it to the states, are reserved to the states respectively, or to the people,"—therefore, also, the same act of Congress, passed on the 14th day of July, 1798, and entitled "An Act for the Punishment of certain Crimes against the United States," as also the act passed by them on the 27th day of June, 1798, entitled "An Act to punish Frauds committed on the Bank of the United States," (and all other their acts which assume to create, define, or punish crimes other than those enumerated in the Constitution,) are altogether void, and of no force; and that the power to create, define, and punish, such other crimes is reserved, and of right appertains, solely and exclusively, to the respective states, each within its own territory.

3. Resolved, That it is true, as a general principle, and is also expressly declared by one of the amendments to the Constitution, that "the powers not delegated to the United States by the Constitution, nor prohibited by

it to the states, are reserved to the states respectively, or to the people;" and that, no power over the freedom of religion, freedom of speech, or freedom of the press, being delegated to the United States by the Constitution, nor prohibited by it to the states, all lawful powers respecting the same did of right remain, and were reserved to the states, or to the people; that thus was manifested their determination to retain to themselves the right of judging how far the licentiousness of speech, and of the press, may be abridged without lessening their useful freedom, and how far those abuses which cannot be separated from their use, should be tolerated rather than the use be destroyed; and thus also they guarded against all abridgment, by the United States, of the freedom of religious principles and exercises, and retained to themselves the right of protecting the same, as this, stated by a law passed on the general demand of its citizens, had already protected them from all human restraint or interference; and that, in addition to this general principle and express declaration, another and more special provision has been made by one of the amendments to the Constitution, which expressly declares, that "Congress shall make no laws respecting an establishment of religion, or prohibiting the free exercise thereof, or abridging the freedom of speech, or of the press," thereby guarding, in the same sentence, and under the same words, the freedom of religion, of speech, and of the press, insomuch that whatever violates either throws down the sanctuary which covers the others,—and that libels, falsehood, and defamation, equally with heresy and false religion, are withheld from the cognizance of federal tribunals. That therefore the act of the Congress of the United States, passed on the 14th of July, 1798, entitled "An Act in Addition to the Act entitled 'An Act for the Punishment of certain Crimes against the United States,'" which does abridge the freedom of the press, is not law, but is altogether void, and of no force.

4. Resolved, That alien friends are under the jurisdiction and protection of the laws of the state wherein they are; that no power over them has been delegated to the United States, nor prohibited to the individual states, distinct from their power over citizens; and it being true, as a general principle, and one of the amendments to the Constitution having also declared, that "the powers not delegated to the United States by the Constitution, nor prohibited to the states, are reserved to the states, respectively, or to the people," the act of the Congress of the United States, passed the 22nd day of June, 1798, entitled "An Act concerning Aliens," which assumes power over alien friends not delegated by the Constitution, is not law, but is altogether void and of no force.

5. Resolved, That, in addition to the general principle, as well as the express declaration, that powers not delegated are reserved, another and more special provision inserted in the Constitution from abundant caution, has declared, "that the migration or importation of such persons

as any of the states now existing shall think proper to admit, shall not be prohibited by the Congress prior to the year 1808." That this commonwealth does admit the migration of alien friends described as the subject of the said act concerning aliens; that a provision against prohibiting their migration is a provision against all acts equivalent thereto, or it would be nugatory; that to remove them, when migrated, is equivalent to a prohibition of their migration, and is, therefore, contrary to the said provision of the Constitution, and void.

6. Resolved, That the imprisonment of a person under the protection of the laws of this commonwealth, on his failure to obey the simple order of the President to depart out of the United States, as is undertaken by the said act, entitled, "An Act concerning Aliens," is contrary to the Constitution, one amendment in which has provided, that "no person shall be deprived of liberty without due process of law;" and that another having provided, "that, in all criminal prosecutions, the accused shall enjoy the right of a public trial by an impartial jury, to be informed as to the nature and cause of the accusation, to be confronted with the witnesses against him, to have compulsory process for obtaining witnesses in his favor, and to have assistance of counsel for his defence," the same act undertaking to authorize the President to remove a person out of the United States who is under the protection of the law, on his own suspicion, without jury, without public trial, without confrontation of the witnesses against him,

SURRENDER OF CORNWALLIS.

without having witnesses in his favor, without defence, without counsel—contrary to these provisions also of the Constitution—is therefore not law, but utterly void, and of no force: That transferring the power of judging any person who is under the protection of the laws, from the courts to the President of the United States, as is undertaken by the same act concerning aliens, is against the article of the Constitution which provides, that "the judicial power of the United States shall be vested in the courts, the judges of which shall hold their office during good behavior," and that the said act is void for that reason also; and it is further to be noted that this transfer of judiciary power is to that magistrate of the general government who already possesses all the executive, and a qualified negative in all the legislative powers.

7. Resolved, That the construction applied by the general government (as is evident by sundry of their proceedings) to those parts of the Constitution of the United States which delegate to Congress power to lay and collect taxes, duties, imposts, excises; to pay the debts, and provide for the common defence and general welfare, of the United States, and to make all laws which shall be necessary and proper for carrying into execution the powers vested by the Constitution in the government of the United States, or any department thereof, goes to the destruction of all the limits prescribed to their power by the Constitution; that words meant by that instrument to be subsidiary only to the execution of the limited powers, ought not to be so construed as themselves to give unlimited powers, nor a part so to be taken as to destroy the whole residue of the instrument; that the proceedings of the general government, under color of those articles, will be a fit and necessary subject for revisal and correction at a time of greater tranquillity, while those specified in the preceding resolutions call for immediate redress.

8. Resolved, That the preceding resolutions be transmitted to the senators and representatives in Congress from this commonwealth, who are enjoined to present the same to their respective houses, and to use their best endeavors to procure, at the next session of Congress, a repeal of the aforesaid unconstitutional and obnoxious acts.

9. Resolved, lastly, That the governor of this commonwealth be, and is, authorized and requested to communicate the preceding resolutions to the legislatures of the several states, to assure them that this commonwealth considers union for special national purposes, and particularly for those specified in their late federal compact, to be friendly to the peace, happiness, and prosperity, of all the states; that, faithful to that compact, according to the plain intent and meaning in which it was understood and acceded to by the several parties, it is sincerely anxious for its preservation; that it does also believe, that, to take from the states all the powers of self-government, and transfer them to a general and consolidated government, without regard to the special government, and reservations solemnly agreed to in that compact, is not for the peace, happiness, or prosperity of these states; and that, therefore, this commonwealth is determined, as it doubts not its co-states are, to submit to undelegated and consequently unlimited powers in no man, or body of men, on earth; that, if the acts before specified should stand, these conclusions would flow from them—that the general government may place any act they think proper on the list of crimes, and punish it themselves, whether enumerated or not enumerated by the Constitution as cognizable by them; that they may transfer its cognizance to the President, or any other person, who may himself be the accuser, counsel, judge, and jury, whose suspicions may

CAPTURE OF STONY POINT.

be the evidence, his order the sentence, his officer the executioner, and his breast the sole record of the transaction; that a very numerous and valuable description of the inhabitants of these states, being, by this precedent, reduced, as outlaws, to absolute dominion of one man, and the barriers of the Constitution thus swept from us all, no rampart now remains against the passions and the power of a majority of Congress, to protect from a like exportation, or other grievous punishment, the minority of the same body, the legislatures, judges, governors, and counsellors of the states, nor their other peaceable inhabitants, who may venture to reclaim the constitutional rights and liberties of the states and people, or who, for other causes, good or bad, may be obnoxious to the view, or marked by the suspicions, of the President, or be thought dangerous to his or their elections, or other interests, public or personal; that the friendless alien has been selected as the safest subject of a first experiment; but the citizen will soon follow, or rather has already followed; for already has a Sedition Act marked him as a prey: That these and successive acts of the same character, unless arrested on the threshold, may tend to drive these states into revolution and blood, and will furnish new calumnies against republican governments, and new pretexts for those who wish it to be believed that man cannot be governed but by a rod of iron; that it would be a dangerous delusion were a confidence in the men of our choice to silence our fears for the safety of our rights; that confidence is every where the parent of despotism; free government is founded in jealousy, and not in confidence; it is jealousy, and not confidence, which prescribes limited constitutions to bind down those whom we are obliged to trust with power; that our Constitution has accordingly fixed the limits to which, and no farther, our confidence may go; and let the honest advocate of confidence read the Alien and Sedition Acts, and say if the Constitution has not been wise in fixing limits to the government it created, and whether we should be wise in destroying those limits; let him say what the government is, if it be not a tyranny, which the men of our choice have conferred on the President, and the President of our choice has assented to and accepted, over the friendly strangers, to whom the mild spirit of our country and its laws had pledged hospitality and protection; that the men of our choice have more respected the bare suspicions of the President than the solid rights of innocence, the claims of justification, the sacred force of truth, and the forms and substance of law and justice. In questions of power, then, let no more be said of confidence in man, but bind him down from mischief by the chains of the Constitution. That this commonwealth does therefore call on its co-states for an expression of their sentiments on the acts concerning aliens, and for the punishment of certain crimes herein before specified, plainly declaring whether these acts are or are not authorized by the federal compact. And it doubts not that their sense will be so announced as to prove their attachment to limited government, whether general or particular, and that the rights and liberties of their co-states will be exposed to no dangers by remaining embarked on a common bottom with their own; but they will concur with this commonwealth in considering the said acts as so palpably against the Constitution as to amount to an undisguised declaration, that the compact is not meant to be the measure of the powers of the general government, but that it will proceed in the exercise over these states of all powers whatsoever. That they will view this as seizing the rights of the states, and consolidating them in the hands of the general government, with a power assumed to bind the states, not merely in cases made federal, but in all cases whatsoever, by laws made, not with their consent, but by others against their consent; that this would be to surrender the form of government we have chosen, and live under one deriving its powers from its own will, and not from our authority; and that the co-states, recurring to their natural rights not made federal, will concur in declaring these void and of no force, and will each unite with this commonwealth in requesting their repeal at the next session of Congress.

NOVEMBER 14, 1798 (SPEECH)

THE REPRESENTATIVES OF THE GOOD people of this commonwealth in general assembly convened, having maturely considered the answers of sundry states in the Union, to their resolutions passed at the last session, respecting certain unconstitutional laws of Congress, commonly called the alien and sedition laws, would be faithless indeed to themselves, and to those they represent, were they silently to acquiesce in principles and doctrines attempted to be maintained in all those answers, that of Virginia only excepted. To again enter the field of argument, and attempt more fully or forcibly to expose the unconstitutionality of those obnoxious laws, would, it is apprehended be as unnecessary as unavailing.

We cannot however but lament, that in the discussion of those interesting subjects, by sundry of the legislatures of our sister states, unfounded suggestions, and uncandid insinuations, derogatory of the true character and principles of the good people of this commonwealth, have been substituted in place of fair reasoning and sound argument. Our opinions of those alarming measures of the general government, together with our reasons for those opinions, were detailed with decency and with temper, and submitted to the discussion and judgment of our fellow citizens throughout the Union. Whether the decency and temper have been observed in the answers of most of those states who have denied or attempted to obviate the great truths contained in those resolutions, we have now only to submit to a candid world. Faithful to the true principles of the federal union, unconscious of any designs to disturb the harmony of that Union, and anxious only to escape the fangs of despotism, the good people of this commonwealth are regardless of censure or calumniation.

Least however the silence of this commonwealth should be construed into an acquiescence in the doctrines and principles advanced and attempted to be maintained by the said answers, or least those of our fellow citizens throughout the Union, who so widely differ from us on those important subjects, should be deluded by the expectation, that we shall be deterred from what we conceive our duty; or shrink from the principles contained in those resolutions: therefore.

RESOLVED, That this commonwealth considers the federal union, upon the terms and for the purposes specified in the late compact, as conducive to the liberty and happiness of the several states: That it does now unequivocally declare its attachment to the Union, and to that compact, agreeable to its obvious and real intention, and will be among the last to seek its dissolution: That if those who administer the general government be permitted to transgress the limits fixed by that compact, by a total disregard to the special delegations of power therein contained, annihilation of the state governments, and the erection upon their ruins, of a general consolidated government, will be the inevitable consequence: That the principle and construction contended for by sundry of the state legislatures, that the general government is the exclusive judge of the extent of the powers delegated to it, stop nothing short of despotism; since the discretion of those who administer the government, and not the constitution, would be the measure of their powers: That the several states who formed that instrument, being sovereign and independent, have the unquestionable right to judge of its infraction; and that

JOHN C. CALHOUN.

MAP OF BOSTON, MASSACHUSETTS, DURING THE AMERICAN REVOLUTION.

a nullification, by those sovereignties, of all unauthorized acts done under colour of that instrument, is the rightful remedy: That this commonwealth does upon the most deliberate reconsideration declare, that the said alien and sedition laws, are in their opinion, palpable violations of the said constitution; and however cheerfully it may be disposed to surrender its opinion to a majority of its sister states in matters of ordinary or doubtful policy; yet, in momentous regulations like the present, which so vitally wound the best rights of the citizen, it would consider a silent acquiescence as highly criminal: That although this commonwealth as a party to the federal compact, will bow to the laws of the Union, yet it does at the same time declare, that it will not now, nor ever hereafter, cease to oppose in a constitutional manner, every attempt from what quarter soever offered, to violate that compact:

AND FINALLY, in order that no pretexts or arguments may be drawn from a supposed acquiescence on the part of this commonwealth in the constitutionality of those laws, and be thereby used as precedents for similar future violations of federal compact; this commonwealth does now enter against them, its SOLEMN PROTEST.

MAIN STREET, YORK, PENNSYLVANIA, WHERE CONGRESS MET, 1777-1778.

The Virginia Resolution

December 24, 1798

☞ Written in secret by moderate Conservative James Madison in 1798.

☞ Referencing the Articles of Confederation, this Resolution was written as a Conservative response to the Left's Alien and Sedition Acts of 1798.

☞ Though he softened the language in his Resolution, Madison reaffirmed Jefferson's essential view (in the Kentucky Resolution) that the Acts overstepped legal boundaries, interfered with states' rights, and represented a congressional "power not delegated by the Constitution."

☞ Madison's Virginia Resolution was passed by the Virginia House of Delegates on December 21, 1798, and by the Virginia Senate on December 24, 1798. But, like Jefferson's Kentucky Resolution, it failed to find approval among the other states. Though the Acts expired after 1800, they remain highly debated and disputed to this day.

R ESOLVED, THAT THE GENERAL ASSEMBLY of Virginia, doth unequivocally express a firm resolution to maintain and defend the Constitution of the United States, and the Constitution of this State, against every aggression either foreign or domestic, and that they will support the government of the United States in all measures warranted by the former.

JAMES MADISON.

That this assembly most solemnly declares a warm attachment to the Union of the States, to maintain which it pledges all its powers; and that for this end, it is their duty to watch over and oppose every infraction of those principles which constitute the only basis of that Union, because a faithful observance of them, can alone secure it's existence and the public happiness.

That this Assembly doth explicitly and peremptorily declare, that it views the powers of the federal government, as resulting from the compact, to which the states are parties; as limited by the plain sense and intention of the instrument constituting the compact; as no further valid that they are authorized by the grants enumerated in that compact; and that in case of a deliberate, palpable, and dangerous exercise of other powers, not granted by the said compact, the states who are parties thereto, have the right, and are in duty bound, to interpose for arresting the progress of the evil, and for maintaining within their respective limits, the authorities, rights and liberties appertaining to them.

That the General Assembly doth also express its deep regret, that a spirit has in sundry instances, been manifested by the federal government, to enlarge its powers by forced constructions of the constitutional charter which defines them; and that implications have appeared of a design to expound certain general phrases (which having been copied from the very limited grant of power, in the former articles of confederation were the less liable to be misconstrued) so as to destroy the meaning and effect, of the particular enumeration which necessarily explains and limits the general phrases; and so as to consolidate the states by degrees, into one sovereignty, the obvious tendency and inevitable consequence of which would be, to transform the present republican system of the United States, into an absolute, or at best a mixed monarchy.

That the General Assembly doth particularly protest against the palpable and alarming infractions of the Constitution, in the two late cases of the "Alien and Sedition Acts" passed at the last session of Congress; the first of which exercises a power no where delegated to the federal government, and which by uniting legislative and judicial powers to those of executive, subverts the general principles of free government; as well as the particular organization, and positive provisions of the federal constitution; and the other of which acts, exercises in like manner, a power not delegated by the constitution, but on the contrary, expressly and positively forbidden by

BRITISH MILITARY GENERAL SIR HENRY CLINTON.

one of the amendments thereto; a power, which more than any other, ought to produce universal alarm, because it is levelled against that right of freely examining public characters and measures, and of free communication among the people thereon, which has ever been justly deemed, the only effectual guardian of every other right.

That this state having by its Convention, which ratified the federal Constitution, expressly declared, that among other essential rights, "the Liberty of Conscience and of the Press cannot be cancelled, abridged, restrained, or modified by any authority of the United States," and from its extreme anxiety to guard these rights from every possible attack of sophistry or ambition, having with other states, recommended an amendment for that purpose, which amendment was, in due time, annexed to the Constitution; it would mark a reproachable inconsistency, and criminal degeneracy, if an indifference were now shewn, to the most palpable violation of one of the Rights, thus declared and secured; and to the establishment of a precedent which may be fatal to the other.

That the good people of this commonwealth, having ever felt, and continuing to feel, the most sincere affection for their brethren of the other states; the truest anxiety for establishing and perpetuating the union of all; and the most scrupulous fidelity to that constitution, which is the pledge of mutual friendship, and the instrument of mutual happiness; the General Assembly doth solemnly appeal to the like dispositions of the other states, in confidence that they will concur with this commonwealth in declaring, as it does hereby declare, that the acts aforesaid, are unconstitutional; and that the necessary and proper measures will be taken by each, for co-operating with this state, in maintaining the Authorities, Rights, and Liberties, referred to the States respectively, or to the people.

That the Governor be desired, to transmit a copy of the foregoing Resolutions to the executive authority of each of the other states, with a request that the same may be communicated to the Legislature thereof; and that a copy be furnished to each of the Senators and Representatives representing this state in the Congress of the United States.

BIRTH OF THE U.S. NATIONAL FLAG, "EMBLEM OF LIBERTY."

The Kentucky Resolution of 1799

1799

☛ Author unknown, though it was clearly inspired by the writings of Conservatives Thomas Jefferson and James Madison.

☛ Written by a Conservative to show continued support for the Kentucky Resolution of 1798, and continued resistance to the Left's unconstitutional Alien and Sedition Acts.

☛ The Kentucky Resolution of 1799 was approved on December 3, 1799.

HOUSE OF REPRESENTATIVES, THURSDAY, NOV. 14, 1799

THE HOUSE, ACCORDING TO THE standing order of the day, resolved itself into a committee of the whole house, on the state of the commonwealth, (Mr. [Robert] Desha in the chair,) and, after some time spent therein, the speaker resumed the chair, and Mr. Desha reported, that the committee had taken under consideration sundry resolutions passed by several state legislatures, on the subject of the Alien and Sedition Laws, and had come to a resolution thereupon, which he delivered in at the clerk's table, where it was read and unanimously agreed to by the house, as follows:

THE KENTUCKY RESOLUTION

The representatives of the good people of this commonwealth, in General Assembly convened, having maturely considered the answers of sundry states in the Union to their resolutions, passed the last session, respecting certain unconstitutional laws of Congress, commonly called the Alien and Sedition Laws, would be faithless, indeed, to themselves, and to those they represent, were they silently to acquiesce in principles and doctrines attempted to be maintained in all those answers, that of Virginia only excepted. To again enter the field of argument, and attempt more fully or forcibly to expose the unconstitutionality of those obnoxious laws, would, it is apprehended be as unnecessary as unavailing.

BATTLE BETWEEN THE FRENCH AND ENGLISH FLEETS.

We cannot, however, but lament that, in the discussion of those interesting subjects by sundry of the legislatures of our sister states, unfounded suggestions, and uncandid insinuations, derogatory to the true character and principles of this commonwealth, have been substituted in place of fair reasoning and sound argument. Our opinions of those alarming measures of the general government, together with our reasons for those opinions, were detailed with decency and with temper, and submitted to the discussion and judgment of our fellow-citizens throughout the Union. Whether the like decency and temper have been observed in the answers of most of those states who have denied, or attempted to obviate, the great truths contained in those resolutions, we have now only to submit

AMERICAN REVOLUTIONARY OFFICER GENERAL ANTHONY WAYNE.

to a candid world. Faithful to the true principles of the federal union, unconscious of any designs to disturb the harmony of that Union, and anxious only to escape the fangs of despotism, the good people of this commonwealth are regardless of censure or calumniation.

Lest, however, the silence of this commonwealth should be construed into an acquiescence in the doctrines and principles advanced, and attempted to be maintained, by the said answers; or least those of our fellow-citizens, throughout the Union, who so widely differ from us on those important subjects, should be deluded by the expectation that we shall be deterred from what we conceive our duty, or shrink from the principles contained in those resolutions,—therefore,

Resolved, That this commonwealth considers the federal Union, upon the terms and for the purposes specified in the late compact, conducive to the liberty and happiness of the several states: That it does now unequivocally declare its attachment to the Union, and to that compact, agreeably to its obvious and real intention, and will be among the last to seek its dissolution: That, if those who administer the general government be permitted to transgress the limits fixed by that compact, by a total disregard to the special delegations of power therein contained, an annihilation of the state governments, and the creation, upon their ruins, of a general consolidated government, will be the inevitable consequence: That the principle and construction, contended for by sundry of the state legislatures, that the general government is the exclusive judge of the extent of the powers delegated to it, stop nothing short of despotism—since the discretion of those who administer the government, and not the Constitution, would be the measure of their powers: That the several states who formed that instrument, being sovereign and independent, have the unquestionable right to judge of its infraction; and, That a nullification, by those sovereignties, of all unauthorized acts done under color of that instrument, is the rightful remedy: That this commonwealth does, under the most deliberate reconsideration, declare, that the said Alien and Sedition Laws are, in their opinion, palpable violations of the said Constitution; and however cheerfully it may be disposed to surrender its opinion to a majority of its sister states, in matters of ordinary or doubtful policy, yet, in momentous regulations like the present, which so vitally wound the best rights of the citizen, it would consider a silent acquiescence as highly criminal: That although this commonwealth, as a party to the federal compact, will bow to the laws of the Union, yet it does, at the same time, declare, that it will not now, nor ever hereafter, cease to oppose, in a constitutional manner, every attempt, from what quarter soever offered, to violate that compact:

BATTLE OF BRANDYWINE.

And finally, in order that no pretexts or arguments may be drawn from a supposed acquiescence, on the part of this commonwealth, in the constitutionality of those laws, and be thereby used as precedents for similar future violations of the federal compact; this commonwealth does now enter against them, its SOLEMN PROTEST.

Extract, etc.
Attest, Thomas Todd, C. H. R.
In Senate, Nov. 22, 1799.——Read and concurred in.
Attest, B. Thurston, C. S.

REVOLUTIONARY WAR SENTINELS.

BY A CONSTITUTION we mean the principles on which a government is formed and conducted.

On the *voluntary* association of men in sufficient numbers to form a political community, the first step to be taken for their own security and happiness, is to agree on the terms on which they are to be united and to act. They form a constitution, or plan of government suited to their character, their exigencies, and their future prospects. They agree that it shall be the supreme rule of obligation among them.

This is the pure and genuine source of a constitution in the republican form. (1825)

William Rawle, Constitutional Scholar

(APPOINTED BY GEORGE WASHINGTON AS U.S. ATTORNEY FOR PENNSYLVANIA)

APPENDIX H

South Carolina's Ordinance of Secession

December 20, 1860

☛ South Carolina: First Southern state to secede from the U.S. Union.

☛ The secession of all 13 Southern states (eleven full, two partial) was prompted by the election of big government Liberal Abraham Lincoln (America's 19th-Century King George III) to the U.S. presidency on November 6, 1860. For he had repeatedly and menacingly suggested that his plan was to further socialize the country and consolidate additional power at Washington.

☛ Note: The ordinance does not mention slavery as a reason for wanting to leave the union; additionally, in his inaugural address Lincoln said he had no desire to interfere with slavery (which was still legal in the North at the time as well). Thus it is obvious that slavery had nothing to do with either Southern secession or the war that followed. South Carolina's ordinance merely asserts that it is dissolving its association with the U.S.—which it, along with the other Conservative Southern states, considered to have grown too large, powerful, Leftist, and tyrannical.

AN ORDINANCE TO DISSOLVE THE Union between the State of South Carolina and other States united with her under the compact entitled "the Constitution of the United States of America."

BATTLE OF SHILOH.

We, the People of the State of South Carolina, in Convention assembled, do declare and ordain, and it is hereby declared and ordained.

That the Ordinance adopted by us in Convention, on the twenty-third day of May, in the year of our Lord one thousand seven hundred and eighty-eight, whereby the Constitution of the United States of America was ratified, and also, all Acts and parts of Acts of the General Assembly of this State, ratifying amendments of the said Constitution, are hereby repealed; and that the union now subsisting between South Carolina and other States, under the name of "The United States of America," is hereby dissolved.[11]

U.S. REVOLUTIONARY GENERAL MARQUIS DE LAFAYETTE AND AMERICAN SPY CHARLES MORGAN.

SURRENDER OF BRITISH COLONEL JOHANN G. RAHL AFTER THE BATTLE OF TRENTON, DECEMBER 26, 1776.

Notes

1. Woods, p. 47.

2. On Lincoln's socialistic, Marxist, and communist thoughts, ideas, and tendencies, see my books: 1) *Lincoln's War: The Real Cause, The Real Winner, the Real Loser*; 2) *Abraham Lincoln Was a Liberal, Jefferson Davis Was a Conservative: The Missing Key to Understanding the American Civil War*; 3) *Abraham Lincoln: The Southern View*. Also see McCarty, passim; Browder, passim; Benson and Kennedy, passim.

3. See J. W. Jones, TDMV, pp. 144, 200-201, 273.

4. See Seabrook, TAHSR, passim. See also, Pollard, LC, p. 178; J. H. Franklin, pp. 101, 111, 130, 149; Nicolay and Hay, ALCW, Vol. 1, p. 627.

5. Seabrook, ASHCSA (J. Davis), p. 59.

6. Seabrook, ASHCSA (J. Davis), pp. 55-56.

7. For more on the nihilistic, atheistic, anti-life, anti-tradition, anti-American, anti-Constitution, anti-capitalism, anti-South agenda of the Victorian Republican Party (then the Liberal Party) and the modern Democrat Party (now the Liberal Party), otherwise known as "The Communist/Socialist Rules for Revolution," see Hasselberg, pp. 2350-2351; Lenin, passim; Marx and Engels, passim; B. Dodd, passim. Also see my book *What the Confederate Flag Means to Me: Americans Speak Out in Defense of Southern Honor, Heritage, and History*. Spring Hill, TN: Sea Raven Press, 2021.

8. *Confederate Veteran*, July 1901, Vol. 9, No. 7, p. 318.

9. For a full examination of the Articles of Confederation see my book: *The Articles of Confederation Explained: A Clause-by-Clause Study of America's First Constitution*.

10. For an in-depth discussion of the Constitution of the Confederate States of America see my book: *The Constitution of the Confederate States of America Explained: A Clause-by-Clause Study of the South's Magna Carta*.

11. For the complete texts of all 13 Southern secession ordinances, as well as a detailed look at Southern secession specifically, see my book: *All We Ask is to be Let Alone: The Southern Secession Fact Book*.

MICHAEL HILLEGASS, AN EDITOR OF THE DECLARATION OF INDEPENDENCE.

AMERICAN REVOLUTIONARY GENERAL FRANCIS "SWAMP FOX" MARION.

AMERICAN REVOLUTIONARY GENERAL, DEFECTOR, AND TRAITOR BENEDICT ARNOLD.

AMERICAN REVOLUTIONARY WAR GENERAL JOSEPH WARREN; DIED AT THE BATTLE OF BUNKER HILL.

AMERICAN REVOLUTIONARY WAR GENERAL RICHARD MONTGOMERY.

SAMUEL HUNTINGTON, FIRST PRESIDENT OF THE U.S. UNDER CONFEDERATION.

Bibliography

READER BEWARE: As is clear from many of the titles I have included in my bibliography, an inordinate amount of them were written by Liberals, socialists, communists, and Marxists, one-sided, error-filled, anti-American works that are of highly questionable value when it comes to the topic of history. Despite this, not only do I own and diligently study such books, I often cite material from them that I believe contributes to an honest understanding of *authentic* history.

Adams, Charles Francis. *The Works of John Adams, Second President of the United States: With a Life of the Author, Notes and Illustrations*. Boston, MA: Little, Brown and Co., 1856.

Alexander, Edward Porter. *Military Memoirs of a Confederate*. New York: Charles Scribner's Sons, 1907

Anderson, Mabel Washbourne. *Life of General Stand Watie: The Only Indian Brigadier General of the Confederate Army and the Last General to Surrender*. Pryor, OK: self-published, 1915.

Armstrong, J. M. *The Biographical Encyclopedia of Kentucky of the Dead and Living Men of the Nineteenth Century*. Cincinnati, OH: J. M. Armstrong and Co., 1878.

Ashe, Samuel A'Court. *History of North Carolina*. 2 vols. Greensboro, NC: Charles L. Van Noppen, 1908.

Bailey, Thomas A. (ed.). *The American Spirit: United States History as Seen by Contemporaries*. Boston, MA: D. C. Heath and Co., 1963.

Benson, Al, Jr., and Walter Donald Kennedy. *Lincoln's Marxists*. Gretna, LA: Pelican, 2011.

Bergh, Albert Ellery (ed.). *The Writings of Thomas Jefferson*. Washington, D.C.: The Thomas Jefferson Memorial Association, 1905.

Bond, P. S. (ed.). *Military Science and Tactics: A Text and Reference for the Reserve Officers' Training Corps*. Washington, D.C.: P. S. Bond Publishing Co., 1938.

Bowen, Catherine Drinker. *John Adams and the American Revolution*. 1949. New York: Grosset and Dunlap 1977 ed.

Boyd, James P. *Parties, Problems, and Leaders of 1896: An Impartial Presentation of Living National Questions*. Chicago, IL: Publishers' Union, 1896.

Broadwater, Jeff. *George Mason: Forgotten Founder*. Chapel Hill, NC: University of North Carolina Press, 2006.

Brock, Robert Alonzo (ed.). *Southern Historical Society Papers*. 52 vols. Richmond, VA: Southern Historical Society, 1876-1943.

Browder, Earl. *Lincoln and the Communists*. New York, NY: Workers Library Publishers, Inc., 1936.

Bryan, William Jennings. *The First Battle: A Story of the Campaign of 1896*. Chicago, IL: W. B. Conkey Co., 1896.

Buchanan, Patrick J. *A Republic, Not an Empire: Reclaiming America's Destiny*. Washington, D.C.: Regnery Publishing, 1999.

Burns, James MacGregor. *The Vineyard of Liberty*. New York, NY: Alfred A. Knopf, 1982.

Carpenter, Stephen D. *Logic of History - Five Hundred Political Texts: Being Concentrated Extracts of Abolitionism; Also Results of Slavery Agitation and Emancipation; Together With Sundry Chapters on Despotism, Usurpations and Frauds*. Madison, WI: self-published, 1864.

Carrington, Henry Beebee. *Battles of the American Revolution, 1775-1781*. New Orleans, LA: A. S. Barnes and Co., 1876.

Christian, George Llewellyn. *Abraham Lincoln: An Address Delivered Before R. E. Lee Camp, No. 1 Confederate Veterans at Richmond, VA, October 29, 1909*. Richmond, VA: L. H. Jenkins, 1909.

——. *A Capitol Disaster: A Chapter of Reconstruction in Virginia*. Richmond, VA: self-published, 1915.

——. *Confederate Memories and Experiences*. Richmond, VA: self-published, 1915.

Coit, Margart L. *John C. Calhoun: American Portrait*. Boston, MA: Houghton Mifflin Co., 1950.

Collier Christopher, and James Lincoln Collier. *Decision in Philadelphia: The Constitutional Convention of 1787*. New York: Ballantine, 1986.

Collier, Thomas S. *The Revolutionary Privateers or Connecticut, With an Account of the State Cruisers, and a Short History of the Continental Naval Vessels Built in the State, With Lists of Officers and Crews*. New London, CT: The New London County Historical Society, 1893.

Confederate Veteran (Sumner Archibald Cunningham, ed.). 40 vols. Nashville, TN: Confederate Veteran, 1893-1932.

Conway, Moncure Daniel (ed.). *The Writings of Thomas Paine*. New York: G. P. Putnam's Sons, 1908.

Curti, Merle, Willard Thorp, and Carlos Baker (eds.). *American Issues: The Social Record*. 1941. Chicago, IL: J. B. Lippincott Co., 1960 ed.

Davidson, Marshall B. *Life in America*. Boston, MA: Houghton Mifflin Co., 1974.

Davis, Jefferson. *The Rise and Fall of the Confederate Government*. 2 vols. New York, NY: D. Appleton and Co., 1881.

Dean, Henry Clay. *Crimes of the Civil War, and Curse of the Funding System*. Baltimore, MD: self-published, 1869.

Dodd, Bella. *School of Darkness*. New York, NY: P. J. Kennedy and Sons, 1954.

Early, Jubal Anderson. *A Memoir of the Last Year of the War for Independence, in the Confederate States of America*. Lynchburg, VA: Charles W. Button, 1867.

Edmonds, George. *Facts and Falsehoods Concerning the War on the South, 1861-1865*. Memphis, TN: self-published, 1904.

Elliot, Jonathan. *The Debates in the Several State Conventions on the Adoption of the Federal Constitution, as Recommended by the General Convention at Philadelphia in 1787*. 4 vols. Washington, D.C.: self-published, 1836.

Ellis, Joseph J. *Founding Brothers: The Revolutionary Generation*. New York: Random House, 2000.

Evans, Clement Anselm (ed.). *Confederate Military History*. 12 vols. Atlanta, GA: Confederate Publishing Co., 1899.

Farrand, Max (ed.). *The Records of the Federal Convention of 1787*. New Haven, CT: Yale University Press, 1911.

Ford, Worthington Chauncey (ed.). *The Writings of George Washington*. New York: G. P. Putnam's Sons, 1891.

Fox, Ebenezer. *The Adventures of Ebenezer Fox, in the Revolutionary War*. Boston, MA: Charles Fox, 1848.

Franklin, John Hope. *Reconstruction After the Civil War*. Chicago, IL: University of Chicago Press, 1961.

Gardiner, C. *Acts of the Republican Party as Seen by History*. Washington, D.C.: self-published, 1906.

Garraty, John A. (ed.). *The American Nation: A History of the United States to 1877*. New York: Harper and Row, 1966.

——. *Historical Viewpoints: Notable Articles From American Heritage*. 2 vols. New York: Harper and Row, 1970.

Godfrey, Carlos E. *The Commander-in-Chief's Guard, Revolutionary War*. Washington, D.C.: Stevenson-Smith Co., 1904.

Goldie, Mark. *John Locke: Two Treatises of Government*. London, UK: Everyman, 1924.

Green, Constance McLaughlin. *Washington: A History of the Capital, 1800-1950*. Princeton, NJ: Princeton University Press,1962.

Greene, Francis Vinton. *The Revolutionary War and the Military Policy of the United States*. New York: Charles Scribner's Sons, 1911.

Groseclose, Tim. *Left Turn: How Liberal Media Bias Distorts the American Mind*. New York: St. Martin's Press, 2011.

Hamilton, Alexander, John Jay, and James Madison (John C. Hamilton, ed.). *The Federalist: A Commentary on the Constitution of the United States*. Philadelphia, PA: J. B. Lippincott and Co., 1877.

Hasselberg, P. D. (ed.). *Parliamentary Debates: First Session, Fortieth Parliament, 1982, House of Representatives* (Vol. 445). Wellington, New Zealand: Government Printer, 1982.

Hunt, Gaillard (ed.). *The Writings of James Madison*. New York: G. P. Putnam's Sons, 1903.

Johnson, Robert Underwood, and Clarence Clough Buel (eds.). *Battles and Leaders of the Civil War*. 4 vols. New York, NY: The Century Co., 1884-1888.

Johnstone, Huger William. *Truth of War Conspiracy, 1861*. Idylwild, GA: H. W. Johnstone, 1921.

Jones, John William. *The Davis Memorial Volume; Or Our Dead President, Jefferson Davis and the World's Tribute to His Memory*. Richmond, VA: B. F. Johnson, 1889.

Kapp, Friedrich. *The Life of Frederick William Von Steuben, Major General in the Revolutionary Army*. New York: Mason Brothers, 1859.

Lenin, Vladimir. *"Left Wing" Communism: An Infantile Disorder*. Detroit, MI: The Marxian Educational Society, 1921.

Livermore, Thomas L. *Numbers and Losses in the Civil War in America, 1861-65*. 1900. Carlisle, PA: John Kallmann, 1996 ed.

Long, E. B., and Barbara Long. *The Civil War Day by Day: An Almanac 1861-1865*. 1971. Cambridge, MA: Da Capo, 1985 ed.

Magliocca, Gerard N. *The Tragedy of William Jennings Bryan: Constitutional Law and the Politics of Backlash*. New Haven, CT: Yale University Press, 2011.

Marx, Karl, and Frederick Engels. *Manifesto of the Communist Party*. Chicago, IL: Charles H. Kerr and Co., 1906.

McAllister, Joseph T. *Virginia Militia in the Revolutionary War*. Hot Springs, VA: McAllister Publishing Co., 1913.

McCarty, Burke (ed.). *Little Sermons in Socialism by Abraham Lincoln*. Chicago, IL: The Chicago Daily Socialist, 1910.

McPherson, James M. *Abraham Lincoln and the Second American Revolution*. New York, NY: Oxford University Press, 1991.

Meriwether, Elizabeth Avery (pseudonym, "George Edmonds"). *Facts and Falsehoods Concerning the War on the South, 1861-1865*. Memphis, TN: A. R. Taylor and Co., 1904.

Miller, Francis Trevelyan, and Robert S. Lanier (eds.). *The Photographic History of the Civil War*. 10 vols. New York, NY: The Review of Reviews Co., 1911.

Minutes of the Eighth Annual Meeting and Reunion of the United Confederate Veterans, Atlanta, GA, July 20-23, 1898. New Orleans, LA: United Confederate Veterans, 1907.

Minutes of the Ninth Annual Meeting and Reunion of the United Confederate Veterans, Charleston, SC, May 10-13, 1899. New Orleans, LA: United Confederate Veterans, 1907.

Minutes of the Twelfth Annual Meeting and Reunion of the United Confederate Veterans, Dallas, TX, April 22-25, 1902. New Orleans, LA: United Confederate Veterans, 1907.

Muzzey, David Saville. *The United States of America: Vol. 1, To the Civil War*. Boston, MA: Ginn and Co., 1922.

——. *The American Adventure: Vol. 2, From the Civil War*. 1924. New York, NY: Harper and Brothers, 1927 ed.

Napolitano, Andrew P. *A Nation of Sheep*. Nashville, TN: Thomas Nelson, 2007.

Neely, Mark E., Jr. *The Fate of Liberty: Abraham Lincoln and Civil Liberties*. Oxford, UK: Oxford University Press, 1991.

Nicolay, John G., and John Hay (eds.). *Abraham Lincoln: A History*. 10 vols. New York, NY: The Century Co., 1890.

——. *Complete Works of Abraham Lincoln*. 12 vols. 1894. New York, NY: Francis D. Tandy Co., 1905 ed.

——. *Abraham Lincoln: Complete Works*. 12 vols. 1894. New York, NY: The Century Co., 1907 ed.

ORA (full title: *The War of the Rebellion: A Compilation of the Official Records of the Union and Confederate Armies*). 70 vols. Washington, DC: Government Printing Office, 1880.

ORN (full title: *Official Records of the Union and Confederate Navies in the War of the Rebellion*). 30 vols. Washington, DC: Government Printing Office, 1894.

O'Shea, M. V. (ed.). *The World Book*. 10 vols. Chicago, IL: W. F. Quarrie and Co., 1922.

Palumbo, Arthur E. *The Authentic Constitution: An Originalist View of America's Legacy*. New York: Algora Publishing, 2009.

Pine, Frank Woodworth (ed.). *Franklin's Autobiography*. New York: Henry Holt and Co., 1912.

Pollard, Edward Alfred. *The Lost Cause*. New York, NY: E. B. Treat and Co., 1867.

Rawle, William. *A View of the Constitution of the United States of America*. Philadelphia, PA: H. C. Carey and I. Lea, 1825.

Richards, Henry Melchoir Muhlenburg. *The Pennsylvania-German in the Revolutionary War, 1775-1783*. Allentown, PA: Pennsylvania-German Society, 1908.

Richardson, John Anderson. *Richardson's Defense of the South*. Atlanta, GA: A. B. Caldwell, 1914.

Roberts, Paul M. *Review Text in United States History*. New York: Amsco School Publications, 1966.

Rogers, William P. *The Three Secession Movements in the United States: Samuel J. Tilden, the*

Democratic Candidate for Presidency; the Advisor, Aider and Abettor of the Great Secession Movement of 1860; and One of the Authors of the Infamous Resolution of 1864; His Claims as a Statesman and Reformer Considered. Boston, MA: John Wilson and Son, 1876.

Rove, Karl. *The Triumph of William McKinley: Why the Election of 1896 Still Matters.* New York, NY: Simon and Schuster, 2015.

Rowland, Kate Mason. *The Life of George Mason, 1725-1792.* New York: G. P. Putnam's Sons, 1892.

Rutherford, Mildred Lewis. *Truths of History: A Fair, Unbiased, Impartial, Unprejudiced and Conscientious Study of History.* Athens, GA: n.p., 1920.

Rutland, Robert Allen. *The Birth of the Bill of Rights, 1776-1791.* 1955. Boston, MA: Northeastern University Press, 1991 ed.

Saffell, William Thomas Roberts. *Records of the Revolutionary War: Containing the Military and Financial Correspondence of Distinguished Officers.* Baltimore, MD: Charles C. Saffell, 1894.

Salley, Alexander Samuel (ed.). *Documents Relating to the History of South Carolina During the Revolutionary War.* Columbia, SC: The State Company, 1908.

Schapiro, Leonard. *The Communist Party of the Soviet Union.* New York: Random House, 1960.

Seabrook, Lochlainn. *Carnton Plantation Ghost Stories: True Tales of the Unexplained from Tennessee's Most Haunted Civil War House!* 2005. Franklin, TN, 2016 ed.

——. *Nathan Bedford Forrest: Southern Hero, American Patriot.* 2007. Franklin, TN, 2010 ed.

——. *Abraham Lincoln: The Southern View.* 2007. Franklin, TN: Sea Raven Press, 2013 ed.

——. *The McGavocks of Carnton Plantation: A Southern History - Celebrating One of Dixie's Most Noble Confederate Families and Their Tennessee Home.* 2008. Franklin, TN, 2011 ed.

——. *A Rebel Born: A Defense of Nathan Bedford Forrest.* 2010. Franklin, TN: Sea Raven Press, 2011 ed.

——. *Everything You Were Taught About the Civil War is Wrong, Ask a Southerner!* 2010. Franklin, TN: Sea Raven Press, revised 2019 ed.

——. *The Quotable Jefferson Davis: Selections From the Writings and Speeches of the Confederacy's First President.* Franklin, TN: Sea Raven Press, 2011.

——. *The Quotable Robert E. Lee: Selections From the Writings and Speeches of the South's Most Beloved Civil War General.* Franklin, TN: Sea Raven Press, 2011 Sesquicentennial Civil War Edition.

——. *Lincolnology: The Real Abraham Lincoln Revealed In His Own Words.* Franklin, TN: Sea Raven Press, 2011.

——. *The Unquotable Abraham Lincoln: The President's Quotes They Don't Want You To Know!* Franklin, TN: Sea Raven Press, 2011.

——. *Honest Jeff and Dishonest Abe: A Southern Children's Guide to the Civil War.* Franklin, TN: Sea Raven Press, 2012.

——. *Encyclopedia of the Battle of Franklin - A Comprehensive Guide to the Conflict that Changed the Civil War.* Franklin, TN: Sea Raven Press, 2012.

——. *The Quotable Nathan Bedford Forrest: Selections From the Writings and Speeches of the Confederacy's Most Brilliant Cavalryman.* Spring Hill, TN: Sea Raven Press, 2012.

——. *Forrest! 99 Reasons to Love Nathan Bedford Forrest.* Spring Hill, TN: Sea Raven Press, 2012.

——. *Give 'Em Hell Boys! The Complete Military Correspondence of Nathan Bedford Forrest.* Spring Hill, TN: Sea Raven Press, 2012.

——. *The Constitution of the Confederate States of America Explained: A Clause-by-Clause Study of the South's Magna Carta.* Spring Hill, TN: Sea Raven Press, 2012 Sesquicentennial Civil War Edition.

——. *The Great Impersonator: 99 Reasons to Dislike Abraham Lincoln.* Spring Hill, TN: Sea Raven Press, 2012.

——. *The Old Rebel: Robert E. Lee As He Was Seen By His Contemporaries.* Spring Hill, TN: Sea Raven Press, 2012 Sesquicentennial Civil War Edition.

——. *The Quotable Stonewall Jackson: Selections From the Writings and Speeches of the South's Most Famous General.* Spring Hill, TN: Sea Raven Press, 2012 Sesquicentennial Civil War Edition.

——. *Saddle, Sword, and Gun: A Biography of Nathan Bedford Forrest for Teens.* Spring Hill, TN: Sea Raven Press, 2013.

——. *The Alexander H. Stephens Reader: Excerpts From the Works of a Confederate Founding Father.* Spring Hill, TN: Sea Raven Press, 2013.

——. *The Quotable Alexander H. Stephens: Selections From the Writings and Speeches of the Confederacy's First Vice President.* Spring Hill, TN: Sea Raven Press, 2013 Sesquicentennial Civil War Edition.

——. *Give This Book to a Yankee! A Southern Guide to the Civil War for Northerners.* Spring Hill, TN: Sea Raven Press, 2014.

——. *The Articles of Confederation Explained: A Clause-by-Clause Study of America's First Constitution.* Spring Hill, TN: Sea Raven Press, 2014.

——. *Confederate Blood and Treasure: An Interview With Lochlainn Seabrook.* Spring Hill, TN: Sea Raven Press, 2015.

——. *Nathan Bedford Forrest and the Battle of Fort Pillow: Yankee Myth, Confederate Fact.* Spring Hill, TN: Sea Raven Press, 2015.

——. *Everything You Were Taught About American Slavery War is Wrong, Ask a Southerner!* Spring Hill, TN: Sea Raven Press, 2015.

——. *Confederacy 101: Amazing Facts You Never Knew About America's Oldest Political Tradition.* Spring Hill, TN: Sea Raven Press, 2015.

——. *The Great Yankee Coverup: What the North Doesn't Want You to Know About Lincoln's War!* Spring Hill, TN: Sea Raven Press, 2015.

——. *Slavery 101: Amazing Facts You Never Knew About America's "Peculiar Institution."* Spring Hill, TN: Sea Raven Press, 2015.

——. *Confederate Flag Facts: What Every American Should Know About Dixie's Southern Cross.* Spring Hill, TN: Sea Raven Press, 2016.

——. *Nathan Bedford Forrest and the Ku Klux Klan: Yankee Myth, Confederate Fact.* Spring Hill, TN: Sea Raven Press, 2016.

——. *Seabrook's Bible Dictionary of Traditional and Mystical Christian Doctrines.* Spring Hill, TN: Sea Raven Press, 2016.

——. *Everything You Were Taught About African-Americans and the Civil War is Wrong, Ask a Southerner!* Spring Hill, TN: Sea Raven Press, 2016.

——. *Nathan Bedford Forrest and African-Americans: Yankee Myth, Confederate Fact.* Spring Hill, TN: Sea Raven Press, 2016.

——. *Women in Gray: A Tribute to the Ladies Who Supported the Southern Confederacy.* Spring Hill, TN: Sea Raven Press, 2016.

——. *Lincoln's War: The Real Cause, the Real Winner, the Real Loser.* Spring Hill, TN: Sea Raven Press, 2016.

——. *The Unholy Crusade: Lincoln's Legacy of Destruction in the American South.* Spring Hill, TN: Sea Raven Press, 2017.

——. *Abraham Lincoln Was a Liberal, Jefferson Davis Was a Conservative: The Missing Key to Understanding the American Civil War.* Spring Hill, TN: Sea Raven Press, 2017.

——. *All We Ask is to be Let Alone: The Southern Secession Fact Book.* Spring Hill, TN: Sea Raven Press, 2017.

——. *The Ultimate Civil War Quiz Book: How Much Do You Really Know About America's Most Misunderstood Conflict?* Spring Hill, TN: Sea Raven Press, 2017.

——. *Rise Up and Call Them Blessed: Victorian Tributes to the Confederate Soldier, 1861-1901.* Spring Hill, TN: Sea Raven Press, 2017.

——. *Victorian Confederate Poetry: The Southern Cause in Verse, 1861-1901.* Spring Hill, TN: Sea Raven Press, 2018.

——. *Confederate Monuments: Why Every American Should Honor Confederate Soldiers and Their Memorials.* Spring Hill, TN: Sea Raven Press, 2018.

——. *The God of War: Nathan Bedford Forrest as He Was Seen by His Contemporaries.* Spring Hill, TN: Sea Raven Press, 2018.

——. *The Battle of Spring Hill: Recollections of Confederate and Union Soldiers.* Spring Hill, TN: Sea Raven Press, 2018.

——. *I Rode With Forrest! Confederate Soldiers Who Served With the World's Greatest Cavalry Leader.* Spring Hill, TN: Sea Raven Press, 2018.

——. *The Battle of Nashville: Recollections of Confederate and Union Soldiers.* Spring Hill, TN: Sea Raven Press, 2018.

——. *The Battle of Franklin: Recollections of Confederate and Union Soldiers.* Spring Hill, TN: Sea Raven Press, 2018.

——. *A Rebel Born: The Screenplay* (for the film). Written 2011. Franklin, TN: Sea Raven Press, 2020.

——. (ed.) *A Short History of the Confederate States of America* (Jefferson Davis, Belford Company, NY, 1890). A Sea Raven Press Reprint. Spring Hill, TN: Sea Raven Press, 2020.

——. (ed.) *Prison Life of Jefferson Davis: Embracing Details and Incidents in his Captivity, With Conversations on Topics of Public Interest* (John J. Craven, Sampson, Low, Son, and Marston, London, UK, 1866). A Sea Raven Press Reprint. Spring Hill, TN: Sea Raven Press, 2020.

——. *What the Confederate Flag Means to Me: Americans Speak Out in Defense of Southern Honor, Heritage, and History*. Spring Hill, TN: Sea Raven Press, 2021.

——. *Heroes of the Southern Confederacy: The Illustrated Book of Confederate Officials, Soldiers, and Civilians*. Spring Hill, TN: Sea Raven Press, 2021.

——. *Support Your Local Confederate: Wit and Humor in the Southern Confederacy*. Spring Hill, TN: Sea Raven Press, 2021.

Simpson, Lewis S. (ed.). *I'll Take My Stand: The South and the Agrarian Tradition*. 1930. Baton Rouge, LA: Louisiana State University Press, 1977 ed.

Skinner, Israel. *A History of the Revolutionary War Between Great Britain and the United States*. Binghamton, NY: self-published, 1829.

Smelser, Marshall. *The Democratic Republic, 1801-1815*. New York: Harper Torchbooks, 1968.

Spaeth, Harold J., and Edward Conrad Smith. *The Constitution of the United States*.1936. New York: Harper Collins, 1991 ed.

Steel, Samuel Augustus. *The South Was Right*. Columbia, SC: R. L. Bryan Co., 1914.

Stephens, Alexander Hamilton. *Speech of Mr. Stephens, of Georgia, on the War and Taxation*. Washington, D.C.: J & G. Gideon, 1848.

——. *A Constitutional View of the Late War Between the States; Its Causes, Character, Conduct and Results*. 2 vols. Philadelphia, PA: National Publishing, Co., 1870.

——. *Recollections of Alexander H. Stephens: His Diary Kept When a Prisoner at Fort Warren, Boston Harbour, 1865*. New York, NY: Doubleday, Page, and Co., 1910.

Thacher, James. *A Military Journal During the Revolutionary War, From 1775 to 1783, Describing Interesting Events and Transactions of This Period*. Boston, MA: Richardson and Lord, 1823.

Thompson, Holland. *The New South: A Chronicle of Social and Industrial Evolution*. New Haven, CT: Yale University Press, 1920.

Thomson, John Lewis. *History of the Indian Wars and War of the Revolution of the United States*. Philadelphia, PA: J. B. Lippincott and Co., 1873.

Trump, Donald, Jr. *Triggered: How the Left Thrives on Hate and Wants to Silence Us*. New York: Center Street, 2019.

United States Library of Congress. Washington, D.C.

United States National Archives. Washington, D.C.

Warner, Ezra J. *Generals in Gray: Lives of the Confederate Commanders*. 1959. Baton Rouge, LA: Louisiana State University Press, 1989 ed.

——. *Generals in Blue: Lives of the Union Commanders*. 1964. Baton Rouge, LA: Louisiana State University Press, 2006 ed.

Watson, Henry Clay. *Camp-fires of the Revolution; or the War of Independence, Illustrated by Thrilling Events and Stories by the Old Continental Soldiers*. Philadelphia, PA: Lindsay and Blakiston, 1856.

Weaver, Addie Guthrie. *The Story of Our Flag: Colonial and National, With Historical Sketch of Betsy Ross*. Chicago, IL: self-published, 1898.

Weintraub, Max. *The Blue Book of American History*. New York: Regents Publishing Co., 1960.

Whipple, Charles King. *Evils of the Revolutionary War*. Boston, MA: New England Non-Resistance Society, 1839.

White, C. Langdon, Edwin J. Foscue, and Tom L. McKnight. *Regional Geography of Anglo-America*. 1943. Englewood Cliffs, NJ: Prentice-Hall, 1985 ed.

Woods, Thomas E., Jr. *The Politically Incorrect Guide to American History*. Washington, D.C.: Regnery, 2004.

Index

MEET THE AUTHOR

NEO-VICTORIAN SCHOLAR LOCHLAINN SEABROOK, a descendant of the families of Alexander Hamilton Stephens, John Singleton Mosby, Edmund Winchester Rucker, and William Giles Harding, is a 7th generation Kentuckian and the most prolific pro-South writer in the world today. Known by literary critics as the "new Shelby Foote" and by his fans as the "Voice of the Traditional South," he is a recipient of the prestigious Jefferson Davis Historical Gold Medal. As a lifelong writer he has authored and edited books ranging in topics from history, politics, science, and biography, to nature, religion, music, and the paranormal; books that his readers describe as "game changers," "transformative," and "life altering."

One of the world's most popular living historians, he is a 17th generation Southerner of Appalachian heritage who descends from dozens of patriotic Revolutionary War soldiers and Confederate soldiers from Kentucky, Tennessee, North Carolina, and Virginia. A proud member of the Sons of the Confederate Veterans, he is a true Renaissance Man. Besides being an accomplished and well respected author-historian and Bible authority, he is also a Kentucky Colonel, eagle scout, screenwriter, nature, wildlife, and landscape photographer, artist, graphic designer, songwriter (3,000 songs), film composer, multi-instrument musician, vocalist, session player, music producer, genealogist, former history museum docent, and a former ranch hand, zookeeper, and wrangler.

His 75 adult and children's books contain some 60,000 well-researched pages that have earned him accolades from around the globe. His works, which have sold on every continent except Antarctica, have introduced hundreds of thousands to vital facts that have been left out of our mainstream books. He has been endorsed internationally by leading experts, museum curators, award-winning historians, bestselling authors, celebrities, filmmakers, noted scientists, well regarded educators, TV show hosts and producers, renowned military artists, esteemed heritage organizations, and distinguished academicians of all races, creeds, and colors. Colonel Seabrook holds the world record for writing the most books on Southern icon Nathan Bedford Forrest: 12.

Of northern, western, and central European ancestry, he is the 6th great-grandson of the Earl of Oxford and a descendant of European royalty. His modern day cousins include: Johnny Cash, Elvis Presley, Lisa Marie Presley, Billy Ray and Miley Cyrus, Patty Loveless, Tim McGraw, Lee Ann Womack, Dolly Parton, Pat Boone, Naomi, Wynonna, and Ashley Judd, Ricky Skaggs, the Sunshine Sisters, Martha Carson, Chet Atkins, Patrick J. Buchanan, Cindy Crawford, Bertram Thomas Combs (Kentucky's 50th governor), Edith Bolling (second wife of President Woodrow Wilson), Andy Griffith, Riley Keough, George C. Scott, Robert Duvall, Reese Witherspoon, Lee Marvin, Rebecca Gayheart, and Tom Cruise.

A constitutionalist and avid outdoorsman and gun advocate, Colonel Seabrook is the author of the international blockbuster, *Everything You Were Taught About the Civil War is Wrong, Ask a Southerner!* He lives with his wife and family in beautiful historic Middle Tennessee, the heart of the Confederacy.

For more information on author Mr. Seabrook visit
LOCHLAINNSEABROOK.COM

SEA RAVEN PRESS

THE WORLD'S #1 SOUTH-FRIENDLY BOOK PUBLISHER

Restoring Dixie's honor
Defending traditional Southern culture
Preserving authentic Confederate history
One book at a time!

Nashville, Tennessee

SeaRavenPress.com

If you enjoyed this book you will be interested in Colonel Seabrook's popular related titles:

☛ THE ARTICLES OF CONFEDERATION EXPLAINED
☛ THE CONSTITUTION OF THE CONFEDERATE STATES OF AMERICA EXPLAINED
☛ ABRAHAM LINCOLN WAS A LIBERAL, JEFFERSON DAVIS WAS A CONSERVATIVE
☛ EVERYTHING YOU WERE TAUGHT ABOUT THE CIVIL WAR IS WRONG, ASK A SOUTHERNER!
☛ ALL WE ASK IS TO BE LET ALONE: THE SOUTHERN SECESSION FACT BOOK
☛ EVERYTHING YOU WERE TAUGHT ABOUT AMERICAN SLAVERY IS WRONG, ASK A SOUTHERNER!

Available from Sea Raven Press and wherever fine books are sold

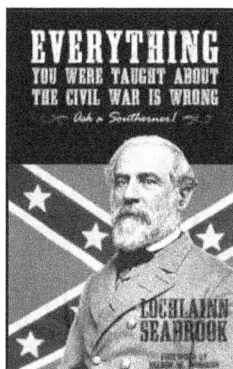

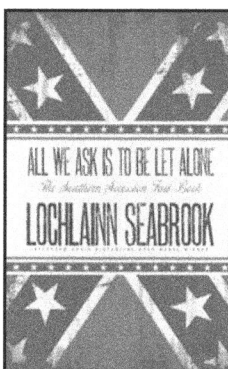

ALL OF OUR BOOK COVERS ARE AVAILABLE AS 11" X 17" COLOR POSTERS, SUITABLE FOR FRAMING

SeaRavenPress.com